THE ... OF JESUS

THE LAST DAYS OF JESUS

MARK 11 TO 16 / DOROTHY LEE

AN ALBATROSS BOOK

the bible reading fellowship
OPENING THE BIBLE

© Commentary: Dorothy A. Lee 1993
© Discussion questions: Albatross Books Pty Ltd 1993

Published in Australia and New Zealand by
Albatross Books Pty Ltd
PO Box 320, Sutherland
NSW 2232, Australia
in the United States of America by
Albatross Books
PO Box 131, Claremont
CA 91711, USA
and in the United Kingdom by
Bible Reading Fellowship
Peter's Way, Sandy Lane West
Oxford OX4 5HG, England

First edition 1993

This book is copyright. Apart from any fair dealing for the purposes of private study, research, criticism or review as permitted under the Copyright Act, no part of this book may be reproduced by any process without the written permission of the publisher.

National Library of Australia
Cataloguing-in-Publication data

Lee, Dorothy A.
The Last Days of Jesus

ISBN 0 7324 1011 8 (Albatross)
ISBN 0 7459 2198 1 (BRF)

1. Jesus Christ – Passion. 2. Bible. N.T. Mark XI–XVI – Commentaries. 3. Passion narratives (Gospels). I. Title.

226.307

Cover photo: John Graham
Printed and bound in Australia by Griffin Paperbacks, Netley, SA

Contents

	Acknowledgements	7
	Introduction	9
1	Jesus enters Jerusalem MARK CHAPTER 11, VERSES 1 TO 33	27
2	Attack and counter-attack MARK CHAPTER 12, VERSES 1 TO 44	43
3	Mark's understanding of the last things MARK CHAPTER 13, VERSES 1 TO 37	68
4	The lead-up to Jesus' arrest: Passover MARK CHAPTER 14, VERSES 1 TO 31	92
5	The agony and arrest of Jesus in Gethsemane MARK CHAPTER 14, VERSES 32 TO 52	114

6 Jesus on trial
MARK CHAPTER 14, VERSE 53 TO
CHAPTER 15, VERSE 20   134

7 The death of Jesus
MARK CHAPTER 15, VERSES 21 TO 47   151

8 The resurrection of Jesus
MARK CHAPTER 16, VERSES 1 TO 8   169

Endnotes   195
Bibliography   207

Acknowledgements

I would like to express my thanks to Graham Hughes of United Theological College, Sydney, who first introduced me to the theology and spirituality of Mark's Gospel. His marvellous lectures still live in my memory and continue to inspire my reading and teaching.

I thank Vicky Balabanski, my colleague and friend, for guiding my footsteps in the treacherous paths of Mark 13 and allowing me access to her PhD thesis.

I thank my husband David Pollard for his unflagging interest and encouragement, and my parents, Edwin and Barbara Lee, for their loving support.

Dorothy A. Lee
December 1993

For:
*My daughters,
Miriam and Irene*

Introduction

THIS BOOK IS A STUDY of the last six chapters of the Gospel of Mark, which narrates the dramatic story of Jesus' last days in Jerusalem (Mark chapters 11 to 16). Beginning with Jesus' entry into Jerusalem, Mark tells of Jesus' conflict with the authorities, his preparation for the passion, his arrest, trial, crucifixion and death, and the discovery of the empty tomb. The Gospel concludes with the women disciples fleeing from the tomb, leaving the story open-ended (chapter 16, verse 8).

Through these events, Mark shares with the reader his theological understanding of Jesus' identity, the significance of Jesus' death, the nature of the kingdom and the meaning of discipleship.

The narrative context (Mark 1 to 10)

The story of Jesus' last days in Jerusalem does not occur in a vacuum. Mark has been preparing his readers all through the Gospel, right from the opening words where he summarises his basic message:

'The beginning of the good news of Jesus Christ, the Son of God' (Mark 1, verse 1). Though it may seem odd, this good news is focussed on the death of Jesus. One writer in 1892 described Mark's Gospel as 'a passion narrative with an extended introduction'.[1] This description is a little over-stated, but it makes an important point: the shadow of the cross looms over the Gospel almost from the start. Although Jesus' impending death is not explicit until Mark 8, verse 31, it has already been hinted at in the first half of the Gospel (see the reference to the bridegroom's departure at chapter 2, verse 20, the plot to kill Jesus at chapter 3, verse 6, and the murder of John the Baptist which prefigures Jesus' death at chapter 6, verses 17 to 29).

Mark's account of the journey from Galilee to Jerusalem (Mark 8, verse 27 to chapter 10, verse 52) deals explicitly with the theme of Jesus' fate in Jerusalem. Three times on the journey, like the solemn tolling of a bell, Mark shows Jesus predicting what is to happen at the journey's end (Mark 8, verse 31; chapter 9, verse 31; chapter 10, verses 32 to 34).[2] While each of these 'passion predictions' includes reference to the resurrection, the focus is on Jesus' passion and death. The notion of suffering, therefore, is central to Mark's narrative and lies at the heart of his theology.

Everything turns on what happens to Jesus in Jerusalem. There, and only there, the kingdom of God — which is the major theme of the Gospel (see

Mark 1, verses 14 and 15) — is brought to fulfilment.

Throughout the journey, the disciples react negatively to Jesus' message of the cross. After each prediction of the passion, the disciples say or do something which shows their lack of understanding (Mark 8, verses 32 and 33; chapter 9, verses 33 to 37; chapter 10, verses 35 to 45). They do not understand why Jesus needs to suffer and die, nor how such suffering originates in and is part of the will of God. They do not understand that the way of the cross is the way of costly discipleship, involving suffering, renunciation and powerlessness (see Mark 8, verses 34 and 35). The whole journey to Jerusalem is focussed on this inability of the inner group of disciples to understand the significance of Jerusalem for Jesus and for their own following of Jesus.

Nevertheless, there are those on the journey (and elsewhere in the Gospel) who do understand Jesus' message. These individuals are, in general, the poor and powerless who have opened themselves to the miracle of faith and the mystery of the kingdom. The 'little people' of the Gospel are epitomised in the two blind men who are healed in the beginning and end of the journey section (Mark 8, verses 22 to 26 and Mark 10, verses 46 to 52). In each case, the miracle of Jesus giving sight to the blind is an image for the life of discipleship.

The illumination of faith is seen to come, not by human effort, but through the power and love of

God. Once we reach Jerusalem, we discover others who have a similar openness to the kingdom and its paradoxical message. In the passion narrative, these disciples include women who understand what seems to elude the inner group, particularly the Twelve.

Thus by the time we reach Jerusalem, we know that Jesus will die by crucifixion at the hands of his enemies. We know that his death is part of God's plan to establish the kingdom and is ordained in scripture. We know that the disciples, particularly the inner circle, have little or no understanding of what Jesus is about in coming to Jerusalem. We also know that, in spite of this, there are some who do understand Jesus' message and who, as faithful disciples, show their love and devotion throughout the tragic events of Jesus' suffering and death.

Mark's passion story: history or theology?

Most students of Mark's Gospel these days believe that Mark was the first Gospel to be written, despite the fact that it follows Matthew in the New Testament canon. It is also probable that Matthew and Luke were dependent on Mark's Gospel. At the same time, they also had access to other sources not found in Mark.

This combination of dependence on Mark and independence from him explains why Matthew and Luke are so similar to Mark in some ways, yet different in others.[3] As we read through chapters 11 to 16 of Mark, you may note some of these similarities and differences. Such a comparison helps us to see what is special and unique about Mark. A comparison with John's Gospel can also be helpful — though John's perspective is very different from the first three Gospels (usually called Synoptic Gospels).

This comparative way of reading the Synoptic Gospels is important if we are to take them seriously. Unfortunately, many Christians are unable to tell the Gospels apart. They have no sense of each Gospel as a separate writing, with its own individual stamp. They harmonise the Gospels to such an extent that, in effect, there is really only one Gospel. It is like giving plasticine to a small child: in no time at all the bright colours have all merged into a dull grey. Or it is like skeins of wool which have become so tangled that it is a frustrating and difficult task to separate them. A better comparison still, it is like getting to know a new member of a family. We may observe the points of family resemblance but, if we are to know that person, we will set aside the rest of the family and attend to that one person in his or her uniqueness.

So also, in reading Mark's story of Jesus, we need to appreciate the narrative in its own right, unravelling the tangled skeins. We need to discover Mark as a unique storyteller and theologian, quite apart from his likeness to the other Gospels.

This point becomes clearer once we realise that Mark is not trying primarily to write history — at least, not in the modern sense.[4] His Gospel is not a modern biography of Jesus, nor is his story of Jesus' last days a 'photographic' or journalistic reproduction of what actually happened. One commentator has described this Gospel as 'a piecing together of stories and sayings in such a way that they constitute an announcement of "the good news"'.[5] Mark is writing about thirty years after the events of Jesus' life (probably in Rome between AD 65 and 75)[6] and his main purpose is to proclaim this 'good news' to a community suffering persecution. This setting shapes profoundly Mark's message. Mark's particular emphases are influenced by the specific context and community out of which his Gospel comes.[7]

Thus, for example, Mark's portrait of the twelve apostles is more negative than that of the other Gospels. Mark is trying to address his Gospel, partly at least, to those who have power in his community and who do not, in his view, have an adequate understanding of the cross. They are too concerned with power and status, too orientated towards achievement and recognition. The portrait of the Twelve says as much about people in Mark's community as it does about the historical group of disciples around Jesus.

In his model of writing about the past which is different from our modern understandings of writing history, Mark allows the past to be shaped by the experience of the present.[8] Thus the Gospel of Mark can be read on more than one historical level: the level of Jesus and his disciples, and the level of Mark and his community.

This is not to say that Mark feels free to manipulate known historical facts, as if he were writing propaganda. Solid history stands behind his Gospel. For example, we know that historically Jesus did truly die on the cross at the hands of the Romans and that this event took place with the support of part, at least, of the Jewish leadership. We know that many of Jesus' closest friends, including Peter, deserted him in his hour of need. We know that Galilaean women disciples found the tomb empty on Easter morning and became convinced, on the basis of their experience, that Jesus had risen from the dead. This is what we may describe as the historical bedrock of Mark's passion story. Such a historical framework is important to our faith, because we believe in a God who intervenes in history and takes seriously our human story.

On the other hand, we need to be careful of imposing a so-called 'scientific' understanding of history onto Mark's Gospel. Each of the four Gospels has its own character, as we have noted, and each tells the story of Jesus in Jerusalem from a different standpoint. Sometimes it is difficult to harmonise all the details and, with our limited understanding this far from the events, there is no point. More important for us is the way each Gospel offers a different theological *interpretation* of Jesus' death. Whether or not we can reconcile the various details in each interpretation is not nearly as important as whether we are prepared to risk living with theological diversity.

The New Testament gives us not one but several different ways of understanding Jesus and the significance of his death and resurrection. If we are to take seriously the New Testament canon, we cannot ignore its diversity or try to squeeze it into our own narrow mould. Just as the person of Jesus Christ, as human and divine, is greater than our feeble attempts to comprehend him, so the same is true of the Gospels. They cannot be neatly categorised in human structures and frameworks. We need to allow Mark's Jesus to address our lives in his uniqueness knowing that, when we read the other Gospels with the same integrity, we will discover yet other facets of the mystery of Jesus.

To sum up so far: history is important in Mark's Gospel, but within a theological rather than scientific-historical, framework. Christians believe that Mark 11 to 16 stands within a reliable historical framework. Yet Mark has his own particular standpoint which gives him perspective with story details which is sometimes different from that of Luke and Matthew and perhaps alien to our modern empirical way of seeing the world.

Mark, in any case, is not writing a history, but a Gospel. He does not present an unbiased, 'objective' account of Jesus' life, death and resurrection. On the contrary, Mark is on Jesus' side from beginning to end: 'Mark's story is written from a standpoint of faith.'[9] The freedom he has to tell the stories of Jesus to reflect his own theological purpose is based on the faith-conviction that the risen Lord is still present in the community for whom he is writing and is not just a figure of the past. Again and again, it is the risen Christ whom we encounter in Jerusalem in Mark's story — as much as it is the historical figure of Jesus of Nazareth.

Past and present come together in Mark's Gospel in a dynamic and creative way.

The traditions behind Mark's story

That Mark is not writing a modern biography of Jesus becomes clearer when we examine the question of the sources behind the Gospel. We have spoken of two levels on which we can read this Gospel: the level of the historical Jesus and the level of Mark's community. Mark's Gospel also gives us insight into a third level, the period between the Easter events and the writing down of the Gospel.

We have learnt a good deal of this period this

century, realising the importance of the oral traditions that lie behind Mark's Gospel. If the Holy Spirit did not whisper directly into Mark's ear (and I do not believe that is how scripture is inspired), then Mark must have gained his information from somewhere else. Many, if not most of the sources he used, would have circulated orally in the early period, rather than in written form.[10]

It is impossible to identify with any certainty the sources behind Mark's Gospel. There is an ancient tradition that Peter was a major source for Mark's story, but this view is not widely accepted.[11] Nevertheless, what we can see are the signs of editing within the Gospel, where one story has been stitched to another (an example of this is the way the story of the fig tree has been joined to the 'cleansing' of the Temple). Some have tried to identify these seams and to guess where the original source began and ended, and how Mark has shaped it. With the passion story, we are dealing with a single narrative which shows the signs of Mark's hand throughout.[12]

More than that we cannot say. Sources cannot easily be detected, due in part to the fact that Mark was such a good editor. He imposed his own stamp on the Gospel and made it a unique and memorable narrative for his community.

Mark's theological perspectives

On the basis of what we have said about history

and theology, and about Mark's editing of sources, we need to ask the question of what is unique in Mark's theological perspective. What are the main points which he is trying to make? How does he shape the traditions which have come down to him and create an intelligible story from them?

Briefly (and these points will recur throughout the book), we can identify three key themes in Mark's Gospel which have shaped the final form of the narrative:[13]

1. *Mark's understanding is essentially a 'theology of the cross'.* Although he believes in the resurrection, Mark locates God's salvation primarily in the death of Jesus. The crucifixion signifies the lowest point of humiliation and powerlessness in Jesus' life. Jesus identifies with the worst in human suffering and misery, embracing fully the human condition. He experiences the agony of death and feels abandoned by everyone, including his Father.

Yet, in a paradoxical way, the absence of God is transformed, through his death, into a life-giving presence. The high point of Mark's Gospel, therefore, is the centurion's affirmation, immediately after Jesus' death: 'Truly, this was God's Son' (Mark 15, verse 39). Here Mark's theology is similar to Paul's understanding of the cross as God's power in weakness, God's wisdom in folly (1 Corinthians 1, verse 18 to chapter 2, verse 5).

Mark's perspective is particularly apposite for a

community suffering persecution and discouraged by failure.

2. *Mark believes that the path of suffering is the path, not only of Jesus' life, but also of the church.* Christians are called, as individuals and as a community, to follow the cross-bearing journey of Jesus to Jerusalem. Not the acquisition of power and status, but the renunciation of power is to be the keynote of Christian living.

This is a perspective which affects all aspects of the church's life. Whether in its spirituality, commitment to social justice or structures of ministry, the church is to live a life of self-denial, renunciation for the sake of the poor, and servanthood. Yet Mark knows that such a call is impossible for human beings by their own effort. Only the miracle of divine grace can transform our human values. Only the power of God can enable us to embrace powerlessness and suffering. It follows, therefore, that the true values of the kingdom are renunciation, openness, vulnerability, and loving service of others.

This is the path by which the church is to proclaim its Lord. It is to respond to the call of costly discipleship.[14]

3. *Mark's understanding of the kingdom is fundamentally an apocalyptic one, a disclosure of God's future, ultimate purpose.* This point is particularly clear in Mark 13. Here the Gospel's apocalyptic language and imagery

become explicit. The kingdom is the key theme of Mark's Gospel and its importance is not lost in the events that take place in Jerusalem. It is a way of speaking of God's final, apocalyptic reign over all things. It refers to God's future, a future beyond history and beyond the limits of human experience. God's kingdom is the reign of God coming out of the future and breaking into the present structures of human existence.

The kingdom thus points to the final victory of God over all evil and suffering. Ironically, such triumph comes not through displays of power, but through suffering and powerlessness. In apocalyptic terms, this suffering is the 'labour pains' which bring to birth the kingdom of God (Mark 13, verse 8).

Thus God's reign is established in a way that undermines human pretensions and structures of power. In the passion narrative, for example, Jesus' crucifixion becomes, in a paradoxical way, a coronation or enthronement. He is proclaimed king in the most humiliating and degrading of circumstances. This is how God's kingdom operates. The glorious and exalted Son of Man, presented with apocalyptic overtones is also, for Mark, the suffering and rejected Son of Man.

Apocalyptic vision and human suffering are welded together in Mark's understanding of the kingdom. God's reign will finally triumph, but in an entirely unexpected way.

Conclusion

The story of Jesus' last days in Jerusalem in Mark's Gospel presents an important challenge for us today. As we gaze on the suffering, crucified One so vividly portrayed in this Gospel, we see reflected there the self-giving God who enters our own pain and the suffering of the world. We are called to a new understanding of what it means to follow such a Lord.

The purpose of Mark's narrative is to bring about conversion in our lives, in an ongoing way, so that we are empowered to take up our cross and follow Jesus. In reading the story of his passion, death and resurrection, we re-discover the suffering Jesus and find in him our true identity. As individuals and as the church, we are to make the apocalyptic journey into Galilee, the place of the end-time, knowing that there in our service of others we will find his risen presence.

Perhaps one of the most vivid contemporary expressions of Mark's theology of the cross, translated into modern idiom, is the hymn of Brian Wren, 'Here hangs a man discarded':

> Here hangs a man discarded,
> a scarecrow hoisted high,
> a nonsense pointing nowhere
> to all who hurry by.

Can such a crown of sorrows
still bring a useful word
where faith and love seem phantoms
and every hope absurd?

Can he give help or comfort
to lives by comfort bound
when drums of dazzling progress
give strangely hollow sound?

Life emptied of all meaning,
drained out in bleak distress,
can share in broken silence
my deepest emptiness;

and love that freely entered
the pit of life's despair
can name our hidden darkness
and suffer with us there.

Lord, if you now are risen,
help all who long for light
to hold the hand of promise
and walk into the night.[15]

Discussion questions

Talking it through

1 Why do the twelve disciples throughout the Gospel of Mark oppose any talk by Jesus of his coming suffering? What point is being made by Mark in showing that the 'little people' have more understanding than the disciples?

2 If Mark's Gospel is not the same as modern historical writing, why is it not propaganda? What is reliable and trustworthy about it?

3 What forms could inspiration have taken in the writing of Mark's Gospel, apart from the Holy Spirit whispering in Mark's ear? What do we actually know about it? What is a reasonable guess?

4 Mark does not simply record past events, but looks back on those events, not merely from his present time, but from a distant future. How does this apocalyptic perspective affect his understanding of the events surrounding Jesus' death?

Introduction/25

Widening our horizons

1 What assumption underlies modern historical writing that is different from that underlying the writing of Mark's Gospel? What important advantage does each type of writing have? What is the danger to the reader in accepting the modern historian's claims on face value?

2 In what sense does a Christian believe that his/her own life has 'apocalyptic significance'? How is this different from delusions of grandeur? How can this sense of partnership with God affect our attitude to:
(a) self?
(b) others?
(c) God?

1
Jesus enters Jerusalem

Mark chapter 11, verses 1 to 33

WITH THE OPENING OF CHAPTER 11, the long journey to Jerusalem — the centre-piece of Mark's Gospel — begins. Jesus' arrival in Jerusalem ushers in a new phase of the Gospel. No longer do we find the peaceful Saviour teaching his disciples about the meaning of suffering, self-denial and being a servant as he does on the road to Jerusalem. Instead, Jesus confronts the old order in a direct and purposeful way, revealing that conflict is of the essence of the kingdom. Of course, conflict has been present almost from the beginning of the Gospel (see, for example, chapter 3, verse 6). Now in the last chapters of Mark's Gospel, it intensifies to a climax.[1]

That Jerusalem is the place of final conflict is appropriate from Mark's point of view. In Jewish and early Christian thinking, Jerusalem was the navel, the centre of the earth. For Mark, the last great battle occurs here, in the religious heart of Israel. Mark is not being anti-Jewish with this view, however. The conflict is an intra-Jewish affair, which Mark interprets in cosmic terms. What takes place in Jerusalem in those fateful last days of Jesus' life determines the universal destiny of the world; everything hinges on it. It is the battle between good and evil, between those who side with the old order of things and those who open themselves to the new — the reign of God revealed in Jesus.

In the light of Jesus' teaching on the journey to Jerusalem about suffering and the renouncing of power, the events of chapter 11 are unexpected, to say the least. First, Jesus enters Jerusalem in apparent triumph and a blaze of glory (verses 1 to 11). Second, he curses the fig tree and 'cleanses' the temple, arousing the fury and indignation of the authorities against him (verses 12 to 25). Third, he enters into hostile dialogue with the authorities concerning the source of his authority (verses 26 to 33). The second section is made up of a frame, one story — the episode of the figtree — wedged within another — the 'cleansing' of the Temple. This is a characteristic of Mark's storytelling.

Here is a plan of the events in this chapter:

I. Triumphal entry into Jerusalem:
Mark 11, verses 1 to 11

* Preparation by two disciples (verses 1 to 6)
* Jesus' entry on the colt (verses 7 to 10)
* Jesus goes to the Temple, then departs (verse 11)

II. The 'cleansing' of the Temple
Mark 11, verses 12 to 25
* Jesus curses the fig tree (verses 12 to 14)
* Jesus 'cleanses' the Temple (verses 15 to 19)
* The fig tree is withered and Jesus explains his action (verses 20 to 25)

III. Questioning of Jesus' authority
Mark 11, verses 27 to 33
* Religious leaders ask, 'By what authority?' (verses 27 and 28)
* Jesus responds with a counter-question (verses 29 and 30)
* Both sides reach an impasse (verses 31 to 33)

I. Triumphal entry into Jerusalem
Mark 11, verses 1 to 11

As Mark tells the story, Jesus' triumphal entry into Jerusalem is not primarily the spontaneous response of the crowd to Jesus' arrival in Jerusalem. In fact, Jesus takes the initiative and sets the whole drama in motion. Mark devotes almost half the narrative to telling how the young donkey is obtained by the two disciples (verses 1 to 6). The emphasis here is on the way that Jesus knows beforehand, and indeed plans for, the event which is about to take place. The donkey is found just where Jesus has foretold and no-one minds the disciples taking it away for his use — again, as Jesus predicts. Jesus is clearly in control of what happens in these events. As one writer has expressed it:

> Here, at the beginning of the Passion narrative, Mark portrays Jesus as the Lord who has everything at his command, including even the donkey of a farmer whom he did not know. The people have correctly perceived Jesus' authority in these events.[2]

The story is vague on details at this point, but it seems likely that the bystanders of verse 5 are the owners of the donkey. At least, they accept responsibility for the animal and recognise the claims of Jesus' authority. The bald words of the two disciples — 'the Lord needs it' (verse 3) — are sufficient to convince the bystanders. It is clear from this that Mark sets the action of this chapter within the context of faith and the recognition of Jesus' authority.

This is a poignant touch. There are very few in the last days of Jesus' life, as Mark tells the story, who possess the faith and insight of these bystanders. Even the inner group of disciples lack this kind of faith. Those who do recognise Jesus' authority, however, are mostly unnamed and all too easily forgotten.

The response of faith continues in the next verses which depict Jesus' ride into Jerusalem acclaimed by the people (verses 7 to 10).[3] There are several points to note about these verses. In the first place, the procession is deeply ironical. On the surface level, it is indeed a 'triumphal' entry. The clothing laid out on the road provides, as it were, a red carpet for Jesus to ride upon (verse 8a); the leafy branches are a sign of celebration, rather as people might wave flags today (verse 8b). The cries of acclamation by the vanguard of the procession and the faithful followers at the back (verses 9 and 10) express the sense of triumph and victory which this entrance celebrates. Jesus is acclaimed as king, and rides into the great city with — apparently — all due pomp and circumstance.[4]

And yet, at the same time, Mark does not allow us to take the story at face value. Yes, we know that what the crowds are saying is true: Jesus' whole ministry has been concerned with 'the coming kingdom of our ancestor, David' (verse 10a). And yes, we know that somehow Jesus' identity as the one 'who comes in the name of the Lord' is central to what the kingdom is about (verse 9b). What we cannot forget, however, in all the extravagance and joy are the solemn words which have tolled like a bell three times on the journey to Jerusalem: 'the Son of Man must suffer many things and be rejected. . .' (chapter 8, verse 31;

chapter 9, verse 31; chapter 10, verses 33 and 34). As readers of the Gospel, we are torn between the sense of joy expressed by the crowds at the coming kingdom and an acute awareness that Jesus has come to Jerusalem to suffer and die. On a deeper level, Jesus' triumphant ride into the city is not a victory procession at all, but a funeral march.

Does this mean that the crowds are wrong in their joyful acclamation of Jesus and the kingdom he brings? Does it mean that Christians each year are wrong to take the story seriously in their celebration of Palm Sunday? The answer to both these questions is No. Mark's purpose is complex in the way he tells the story.

On the one hand, he is trying to undermine the popular belief in a triumphant, victorious ruler who achieves victory through power and display. This is precisely what Jesus does *not* do in Mark's Gospel — as we will see more clearly as we move through the passion story. Mark's Jesus is the one who has spoken throughout the journey to Jerusalem about giving up wealth and power and dominance over others (chapter 8, verses 34 to 37; chapter 9, verses 33 to 37; chapter 10, verses 17 to 27, 35 to 45). His ministry has called for self-denial and taking up the cross, not nationalistic fervour and Israel's military triumph.

God is to bring about the kingdom in a way that is radically different from what the crowd expects:

The reconstruction of Israel's past glories is not the way that God will come to his people to deliver them. That will be brought about through the humble service and total renunciation of Jesus.[5]

On the other hand, there is a deeper truth contained in the words of the crowds in their acclamation of Jesus, which Mark wishes his readers to grasp. They are not entirely wrong to rejoice, even though they do not see the cross that lies ahead and even though they, too, will play their part in calling for Jesus' crucifixion (chapter 15, verses 11 to 14). Here, the cries of 'Hosanna' (see Psalm 118, verses 25 and 26) and the waving of branches are part of the ritual of the Feast of Booths (or Tabernacles) — which is, at least in part, a celebration of God's liberation in the Exodus (see Leviticus 23, verses 39 to 43 and Deuteronomy 16, verses 13 to 15).[6]

God's liberating salvation is ultimately what Jesus' entry into Jerusalem is all about and that is certainly a cause for joy. However, it is a salvation which is achieved not through power, but through suffering. In this sense, Mark's story of Jesus' entry into Jerusalem overturns the expectations of the reader. Although it appears at first to be a story of triumph and achievement, the real message is the opposite: not power, but powerlessness; not triumph as the world knows it, but resurrection which is won only at the cost of suffering and death.

II. The 'cleansing' of the Temple
Mark 11, verses 12 to 25

As we noted at the beginning, Mark deliberately frames the story of Jesus in the Temple with the cursing of the fig tree. The story of Jesus cursing a perfectly innocent tree because it has failed to bear fruit out of season is a difficult one to understand — especially for those conscious of ecological issues! However, to ask why Jesus might have done such a senseless thing is to ask the wrong question. Our concern is not primarily with what Jesus might have said and done, but rather with how Mark has shaped and interpreted these events.

The real question we need to ask, therefore, is why Mark has placed the story in this context. Elsewhere in the Gospel, Mark uses such a framing device (e.g. the story of Jairus' daughter and the woman with a haemorrhage in chapter 5, verses 21 to 43) in order to set one story in close relationship to another. In other words, we can only understand the fig tree in relation to the incident in the Temple. The one story helps us to interpret the other; the two can only be understood together.

Operating on this principle, we begin by examining the Temple story (verses 15 to 19). Traditionally this story has been called a 'cleansing' — that is, Jesus enters the Temple, finds activity going on there which he considers disrespectful and dishonest, and so purifies it by driving out the offenders.[7] But is that really what Mark is on about? The only explanation Mark gives in these verses is the Old Testament quotation in verse 17 ('My house shall be called a house of prayer for all the nations', Isaiah 56, verse 7) to which are added the final words ('den of robbers') from Jeremiah 7, verse 11. Here, Jesus is objecting to the Temple being used as a trading place instead of a place of prayer. How does this help us understand Jesus' actions in verses 15 to 16?

It is at this point that the incident of the fig tree becomes relevant. However irrational it may seem from a modern point of view, the story represents Jesus' judgment on the fig tree for being unproductive and unfruitful (see Jeremiah 8, verse 13; Ezekiel 17, verse 24; Joel 1, verse 7; and Luke 13, verses 6 to 9). The real significance of Mark's story now begins to emerge. Jesus' problem with the Temple is that, like the fig tree, it has not borne fruit. Despite being 'an emblem of peace and prosperity' in the Old Testament, the fig tree has proved barren and infertile.[8] In the same way, the Temple has failed to be a house of prayer and has turned instead into something evil and destructive.

The story of the cursing of the fig tree, therefore, has two functions. First, it is an attack on the Temple system and the Temple authorities for their failure to produce the fruits of Israel's harvest. Second, Jesus' actions in clearing the Temple signify, for Mark, not a cleansing renewal, but the pronouncement of judgment against the Temple and its power structures. Though built as the centre of worship for all peoples — Jew and Gentile alike — the Temple, in Mark's view, now represents the old order of things, the structures of power and domination on which the kingdom passes judgment. In this sense, the story of the 'cleansing' of the Temple is really a story about judgment and not about cleansing and renewal at all.[9]

If this is the case, if may be asked what connection the following sayings on faith, prayer and forgiveness have to do with what has gone before (verses 22 to 26). The link seems to be a loose one. Jesus is speaking here of the power of prayer to achieve what is humanly impossible. This is a characteristic Markan theme (e.g. see chapter 9, verse 29). It is linked both to the entry into Jerusalem and to the 'cleansing' of the Temple, all three of which have a common focus on faith and prayer.

Mark is saying that, even without the Temple, God's power is still available to those who pray where there is true faith. This is also true of the forgiveness of sins (verse 25), traditionally associated with the Temple ritual.

III. Questioning of Jesus' authority
Mark 11, verses 27 to 33
As a result of the attack on the Temple, the authorities now react by asking Jesus what right he

has to act in so outrageous and unprecedented a manner (verse 28). What is the nature of the power that lies behind his actions?

Earlier in the Gospel, the authorities have already accused Jesus of being driven by the power of Satan in his ministry of healing and forgiving (chapter 3, verses 22 to 27). Clearly, therefore, the question in Mark 11 is not a genuine question at all. It is a negative challenge to Jesus which is itself the expression of unbelief. Nevertheless, it reveals that the basic issue behind the conflict between Jesus and the establishment is that of authority.[10]

Recognising their motivation, Jesus answers the authorities' question with one of his own, which puts them in a double bind. He asks them to name the source of John the Baptist's authority to baptise (verse 30). At once, they perceive the trap. They cannot say anything positive about John the Baptist because of his link with Jesus; nor can they speak disparagingly of John because of the high regard in which he is held by the people (verses 31 and 32).

For the moment, the conflict reaches a stalemate. The authorities are foiled in their attempt to discredit Jesus, while Jesus is not prepared to expose himself to their hostility any more than is necessary.

Conclusion

Mark has presented us in this chapter of the Gospel with three stories which set the tone for Jesus' last days in Jerusalem. Jesus is clearly the aggressor in these stories. His ride into Jerusalem and his dramatic actions in the Temple provoke an outraged hostility from the authorities. Jesus enters the lions' den and confronts his opponents face-to-face.

For Mark, these powers represent the forces of evil, the structures of the old order which God's power challenges and finally overthrows. There is nothing weak or impotent about Mark's understanding of the kingdom. The reign of God has a kind of ferocity within it, a fire that burns its way into the very heart of evil. Jesus' provocative actions are the first round in the conflict between the powers of the old and the powers of the new.

There is a paradox within all of this, however, which is apparent in a comparison of the first two stories in this chapter of the Gospel. The entry into Jerusalem, with its ironical undertones, serves — at least in part — to undermine a human understanding of power. It is a reminder to us that the power of the gospel is won through suffering, powerlessness and vulnerability. The 'cleansing' of the Temple, on the other hand, asserts unequivocally the power and might of the kingdom over against the forces of evil.

Can these two perspectives be reconciled or is each speaking out of a different framework? Does the kingdom come through power or through powerlessness, through force or through suffering?

The answer to this question is not revealed until

the end of the Gospel. Nevertheless, one point can be made at this stage of the narrative. The power and forcefulness of Jesus' actions in the Temple are important, but do not finally bring the kingdom to birth. Though they point to God's ultimate intention to overthrow evil, they lead — at least, from a human point of view — to suffering, humiliation and death. In the final analysis, Jesus' actions yield before a greater power and a greater mystery which for Mark lies at the heart of the kingdom: the power of self-giving and suffering.

This paradoxical dynamic of conflict and triumph achieved only through suffering and death is captured in the last stanzas of Henry Hart Milman's Palm Sunday hymn:

> Ride on, ride on in majesty;
> your last and fiercest strife is nigh;
> the Father on his sapphire throne
> awaits his own anointed Son.
>
> Ride on, ride on in majesty,
> in lowly pomp ride on to die;
> bow your meek head to mortal pain,
> then take, O God, your power and reign!

Discussion questions

Talking it through

1 How does Mark mean Jesus' entry into Jerusalem in triumph (verses 1 to 11) to be understood? How does this understanding turn our normal conception of such an event upside down?

2 How are the cursing of the fig tree and the 'cleansing' of the Temple linked? How do these stories continue the theme begun by Mark in the triumphant entry into Jerusalem?

3 Mark is a storyteller rather than a systematic theologian. How does his presentation of each of the following indicate the power of the good storyteller:
(a) his presentation of Jesus' conflict with the authorities (verses 27 to 33)?
(b) Jesus' cleansing of the Temple (verses 15 to 19)?
Does the story in each of these cases enhance or impede Mark's essential message?

4 What sort of person does Mark reveal Jesus to be? How does he bring these characteristics out? What is the value to us of seeing that Jesus is this sort of person?

Widening our horizons

1 In this chapter, we see Jesus not simply waiting for the inevitable, but taking the initiative. What initiatives could we take in the following situations:
(a) the way we care for someone with a wasting terminal disease?
(b) the way we respond to a corrupting work environment?
(c) the way we respond to the gradual breakdown of our marriage?

What are worthwhile principles to bear in mind in such cases?

2 The picture that Mark gives of Jesus here, as elsewhere, is that Jesus objects to the sorts of earthly power structures the Temple authorities, for instance, represent — that serve the ambitions of humankind rather than the purposes of God. What features of the following organisations do you feel Jesus would be unhappy about:
(a) the modern nation-state?
(b) the church as we know it?
(c) the modern corporation?

2
Attack and counter-attack

MARK CHAPTER 12, VERSES 1 TO 44

THE HOSTILITY WHICH WE SAW in the last chapter of Mark's Gospel escalates as a result of Jesus' action in the Temple. What follows is a series of verbal confrontations between Jesus and the religious leaders.

It begins with the parable of the vineyard which, as Mark interprets it, is a direct attack by Jesus on the authorities. This is followed by three theological questions. The first two are attempts by various groups to entrap Jesus and discredit him with the people. The third question comes from the same source, but breaks the pattern of hostility and malice in an unexpected way.

44/Attack and counter-attack

Finally, the chapter concludes with Jesus' counter-attack against the leaders for their ignorance and oppression of the poor. By the end of this chapter, it becomes clear that the authorities are unable to silence Jesus or defeat him in theological debate. They have no option left but to resort to violence.

The chapter falls naturally into three parts. The first and third sections represent Jesus' attack on the authorities. The middle section is the authorities' attack on Jesus, which is itself in three sub-sections:

I. The parable of the vineyard and the tenants
Mark 12, verses 1 to 12
* The parable (verses 1 to 9)
* The interpretation of the parable (verses 10 and 11)
* The response of the authorities (verse 12)

II. Authorities direct three questions to Jesus
Mark 12, verses 13 to 34
* Paying taxes to Caesar: Pharisees and Herodians (verses 13 to 17)
* Marriage in the resurrection: Sadducees (verses 18 to 27)
* The greatest commandment: a scribe (verses 28 to 34)

III. Jesus' counter-attack against the scribes
Mark 12, verses 35 to 44)
* Jesus' question about David's Son (verses 35 to 37)

* Jesus denounces the scribes: warnings (verses 38 to 40)
* example of the widow (verses 41 to 44)

I. The parable of the vineyard and the tenants
Mark 12, verses 1 to 12

As we saw in the previous chapter, the first round of conflict in Jerusalem has gone to Jesus. The second round opens with a parable which, in Mark's telling, is addressed directly to the religious authorities. At one level, the parable is a simple story based on everyday life in Palestine in a rural and agricultural context. It is on that level that we need to begin hearing the parable, setting aside for the moment its religious and theological implications with which we are all familiar.

The parable is structured around a simple plot:

❑ *The scene is set (verse 1)*

The owner of the vineyard, having dug out, cultivated and in every way prepared his vineyard, then departs, leasing the land to tenant farmers. The agreement with the tenants is that they farm the vineyard on his behalf, keeping a percentage of the profits for themselves and harvesting the rest for the owner. He is an absentee landlord, a common enough phenomenon in the Palestine of Jesus' day.

❏ *Harvest time: sending the servants (verses 2 to 5)*
When it is time for harvest, the owner sends a servant to collect the rent. At this point, the story begins to go awry. Instead of handing over the produce of the vineyard, the tenant farmers beat up the servant and send him back empty-handed (verse 2). Then follows a similar series of incidents: the owner sends more slaves and the violence escalates from physical assault to murder (verses 3 to 5). The legal contract between owner and tenants has been broken in the most brutal of ways.

❏ *Harvest time: sending the son (verses 6 to 8)*
The listener's curiosity is now aroused. How will the owner respond to the tenant farmers? He has exhausted his options and lost servants in the process. Will he give up on the vineyard and leave it in the hands of these violent squatters? Or will he seek an instant and bloody revenge?

What he does comes as a surprise. He decides to send his son instead, arguing that the murderers will show a respect for the son which they have not shown his servants (verse 6). The owner's naivety here increases dramatically the narrative tension. We know that he is taking a terrible risk and that the situation is ripe for tragedy. Moreover, the decision is made more poignant by the fact that the son is described as 'beloved' to the owner (verse 6) and is his only son, the heir to the property (verse 7).

And our anxiety is justified. The owner's action

gives the murderers the opportunity they seek to take permanent possession of the vineyard (verse 7). The worst happens. The fate of the servants becomes the fate of the only son and his murdered body is flung contemptuously over the vineyard wall, unburied (verse 8).[1]

The last part of the story is couched as a question to the hearers (verse 9a). Now we are speaking of the future and have moved outside the parable into dialogue with the audience. These verses express our sense of justice. We know what *ought* to happen; we know that in an ideal world murderers do not get away with such brutality. The vineyard, therefore, will be taken from the wicked tenant farmers and given to other tenants.

For Mark, this dialogue relates to what has just taken place in the 'cleansing' of the Temple. There, the theme has been judgment on the religious structures and leadership of the Temple. The Temple is to be replaced by the new community of prayer and discipleship centred around Jesus (see also chapter 3, verses 31 to 35).

In the following verses, Mark adds further interpretation to the parable. The story is related directly to Jesus' own experience in Mark's Gospel (verses 10 and 11). Quoting Psalm 118, verses 22 and 23 (the same Psalm quoted at chapter 11, verse 9 in the triumphal entry), Jesus is identified with the rejected son in the parable. Yet his rejection is somehow at the centre of God's saving plan. The parable here is an allegory for God's relationship with Israel and many of the elements in the story correspond to theological points. Thus Israel is the vineyard, God is the owner, the religious authorities are the tenant farmers, the prophets are the servants and Jesus is the only son who is murdered.

Yet not all the details fit and we need to be wary of this kind of treatment of Jesus' parables. In many cases, the allegory is a later interpretation which in some ways is different from Jesus' original intention in telling the parable. For example, God cannot be equated with an absentee landlord. Nor does God naively send Jesus without any idea of what might happen to him.

Similarly, Jesus is not killed by stoning and thrown out of the city unburied. On the contrary, he is killed by the Romans by crucifixion and he is given a rich burial by Joseph of Arimathaea (Mark 15, verses 43 to 46; see also John 19, verses 38 to 42).

All this means that we need to realise here, as elsewhere, that Mark is not just telling the story exactly the way Jesus told it. Mark is re-telling Jesus' parable (as he also does at chapter 4, verses 1 to 34), drawing out more fully its meaning in the light of Jesus' death and resurrection. The Gospel of Thomas, which is not part of the New Testament, tells the same parable in a simpler way:

There was a good man who owned a vineyard.
He leased it to tenant farmers so that they might
work it and he might collect the produce from
them. He sent his servant so that the tenants
might give him the produce of the vineyard.
They seized his servant and beat him, all but killing him. The servant went back and told his
master. The master said, 'Perhaps they did not
recognise him.' He sent another servant. The
tenants beat this one as well. Then the owner
sent his son and said, 'Perhaps they will show
respect to my son.' Because the tenants knew
that it was he who was the heir to the vineyard,
they seized him and killed him.[2]

It is quite likely that this is a very early version of the story as told by Jesus.[3] If we compare it to Mark's version, we can see how the church has developed the ideas in it and made it into an allegory of salvation.[4]

This need not be seen as a bad thing. Mark and his community realised that Jesus' parable had more to it than previously thought. They drew out the meaning to make it more relevant to Jesus' own experience in the events of Easter. We now read it through Mark's eyes as a story which is basically about Jesus being sent by God and rejected by the religious leaders. We read it now as part of the Easter story. The primary focus, for Mark, is on the death of Jesus, although (in verses 10 and 11) there is a strong hint to Christian readers of the resurrection.[5]

The authorities know full well that the parable is a direct attack on them (verse 12). Despite their desire to lay hands on Jesus — thus fulfilling the parable (see verse 8) — they are prevented from doing so out of fear of the crowds who are enthusiastic about Jesus and eager to hear his teaching (see verse 37). The crowd unwittingly provides a protective barrier around Jesus. The question in the reader's mind, therefore, is whether and how the authorities will succeed in their desire to lay violent hands upon Jesus.

For the moment, the leaders are thwarted. We know, however — from the parable, if from nowhere else — that they will not be frustrated for ever. Sooner or later, they will achieve their ends.

II. Authorities direct three questions to Jesus
Mark 12, verses 13 to 34

The next ploy of the authorities is to discredit Jesus' teaching in the eyes of the crowds. A series of three difficult and controversial questions are now presented to Jesus for his response. As is so often the case in a series of threes, however, the third is very different from the first two.

Despite the different content, the first two questions have a similar format: the group begins by asking a question which is a controversial one, either for political or theological reasons, and which centres on a dilemma of some kind; Jesus is expected to solve the problem. The first question is explicitly described as a trap (verse 13) and the second belongs probably in the same category. In each case, Jesus manages to give a lucid and intelligent answer without being trapped in the dilemma.

The first question is asked by a coalition of Pharisees and Herodians. Not much is known of the Herodians. It is likely, however, that what we find here is an unholy alliance. The Pharisees, who are pro-Jewish and anti-Roman, are teaming up with members of Herod Antipas' party which is pro-Roman and only marginally Jewish. Significantly, these two groups have already joined hands in the Gospel at chapter 3, verse 6 — again in the context of shared hostility towards Jesus and the determination to get rid of him. This is enough to show that the question is a conspiracy between the two groups, without Mark even having to tell us so.

The question presented to Jesus centres on the relationship between the Jewish people and the hated Roman overlords. It is focussed on the emotive and controversial issue of taxation, particularly the payment of the poll-tax. The idea is to trap Jesus either into a pro-Roman statement, thus alienating the crowds, or into an anti-Roman statement, thus alienating the Romans. Jesus neatly sidesteps the alternatives presented to him, just as he has done with the religious leaders over the question of authority (chapter 11, verses 29 to 32). In this case, Jesus does not say, 'I don't know', as the authorities have done. Instead he gives an ambiguous answer, using a Roman coin, which says that people need to give to God and to Caesar what is owed to each.[6]

Does Jesus advocate the payment of taxes to the Romans, including the hated poll-tax? Many writers have suggested that Jesus is separating our responsibilities to God from our responsibilities to the state and the secular powers. Others have argued that Mark is reminding us, as Christians, that we need to obey the civil powers, whether we like paying our taxes or not. There are problems with both these interpretations. In the first place, no good theology (and Mark is a good theologian) separates responsibilities to God from responsibilities to others. God is sovereign over all things and over every aspect of our lives.[7] Everything we are and do is relevant to our relationship with God.

In the second place, it is unlikely that this passage is speaking of the powers of the state which we as citizens should respect at all costs. It was this view which (at least in part) tragically misled much of the German church to support Hitler and Nazism in the 1930s and 1940s. Jesus' context, and also Mark's, is that of the oppressive rule of Rome, uninvited and unwanted by the people of the land. It led to the devastation of Jerusalem and the Temple, and the massacre of countless Jews in the Jewish War (AD 66 to AD 73). Mark is not suggesting that the people are obliged to pay the Roman poll-tax. Nor is he advocating violent and bloody resistance to Roman power, as the Zealots wanted. Caesar's power is answerable to God and, in as much as it upholds tyranny and oppression, it stands over against God and God's kingdom.[8]

Jesus' answer, therefore, leaves open the question of whether or not to pay the poll-tax. The point is that behind the narrow political agenda lies the larger and more fundamental question of the relationship between God's power and Caesar's power, and how the one operates in relation to the other. How we act today in response to this and to similar questions will depend entirely on our own context. There is no quick answer, or ready-made formula, to the deep political and human questions of our society.[9] What is important is that we respond in the light of God's kingdom and refuse to be imprisoned in ideological agendas, whether political or theological.

The second question is not nearly as complex as the first (verses 18 to 27). This time, it is the Sadducees who bring a question. The Sadducees were a major party within the Judaism of Jesus' day, particularly associated with the ruling class and Temple élite in Jerusalem. They seem to have believed that only the first five books of the Bible (the Pentateuch or Torah) were important. Therefore, among other things, the Sadducees did not believe in the resurrection of the dead, but held to the older Jewish view of a vague and shadowy existence in Sheol — the place where the dead were thought to go. The question is an attempt to trap Jesus by showing how ridiculous the notion of resurrection is.

The story they tell is not quite as absurd in the ancient Jewish world as it is today. The Sadducees are referring to the law of 'levirate marriage' in the Old Testament by which a brother-in-law was expected to marry his sister-in-law if the brother died childless, in order to raise up children to his brother's line (see Deuteronomy 25, verses 5 to 10).[10] Jesus answers the Sadducees in their own terms by quoting from the Pentateuch (Exodus 3, verses 6, 15 and 16). There, he argues, it is assumed that God is *still* the God of Israel's ancestors even after they have died. At this point (ironically) Jesus is upholding a doctrine which the Pharisees also support.

In many respects, the third question is the most interesting of all (verses 28 to 34). As Mark tells the story, the pattern is broken: the scribe who asks the next question is not attempting to trap Jesus but, on the contrary, is impressed by Jesus' answers thus far.[11] The question he asks is one of the most important religious questions and certainly a fundamental question for Jews, educated in the Law or Torah: 'Which commandment is the first of all?' What, in other words, is the most important aspect of the faith, if it were to be summarised in a few words?

Jesus' answer comes straight from the Torah (Exodus 6, verse 4) and is a summary of the Ten Commandments. It is so Jewish an answer that it reminds us Christians of something we forget, something implicit in Mark's story: how very Jewish Jesus was and how Jewish his faith. The centre of true religion, says Jesus — and this is as true for Christian as for Jewish faith — lies in an authentic love of God and an equally authentic love of others.[12]

In both cases, however, we are told a little more about how we are to love. Our love for God is to be a love of the whole person: a love which comes from the heart, which influences the will and which exercises the mind. It is to be a holistic love, embracing body and spirit, intellect and emotions. The love of God is to be the centre of our lives, that which we long for and strive towards more than anything else.

Our love for others is also qualified, though in a different way. It is to be as intense and committed as our love for ourselves. It is important that we hear the implications of this command: it assumes that we *do* have an authentic sense of self-love. People sometimes need to be reminded of this point. We are often reproved in the church for being selfish and self-centred. But not everyone suffers from this form of sin — or at least not to the same extent. Some people are loving and self-giving to others, but at the cost of putting themselves down and under-valuing their own gifts.[13]　Others have neither true self-love, nor love for others.

The second commandment, in other words, has two dimensions: love of others and love of self. Both are equally necessary for true faith. Christian humility ought not to be confused with the tendency to demean ourselves and the failure to nurture and care for ourselves. Self-love is an intrinsic part of the command of God. We are valuable in God's eyes for who and what we are — with all our inadequacies — and we need to learn to love ourselves as God does. This universal love which the Old Testament and Jesus call us to embrace excludes no-one, least of all ourselves!

The two commands — to love God and to love others — cannot therefore be separated. Though they are in one sense different and are not the same thing, they belong together. The one needs to flow into the other. As one writer has put it, commenting on the second commandment in relation to the first:

> . . . to love God out of a whole heart is to be free and courageous in fulfilling the will of God in our relationships with our fellow human beings and with ourself. To love God out of our whole soul is to open ourselves to actualising the possibility and freedom of God in all levels of human society. To love God out of a whole mind is to employ all the powers of the intellect in devotion to the creator by discovering new

and superior ways of building social and economic institutions that eliminate poverty, ignorance and disease.[14]

If our love of God is not accompanied by a deepening love for ourselves, for others and a stronger commitment to justice, then it is not an authentic love. Similarly, a love of others which is not grounded ultimately in the love of God — even though we may not express it in those terms — is neither sustainable, nor sufficiently radical to encounter the tragic realities of human suffering. Only the sense of a transcendent meaning and the belief in 'the mystery at the heart of things' gives us the hope and motivation to love others in the same way we love ourselves.

The scribe is impressed with Jesus' answer and endorses it enthusiastically. His additional words about sacrifices and burnt offerings (verses 32 and 33) reinforce the point: love of God and love of neighbour are what true sacrifice is all about. (This is seen, above all, in the life and death of Jesus whose love of God and others is at the heart of his life and death.)

Jesus is moved by the scribe's enthusiasm and affirms his response with warmth and admiration: 'You are not far from the kingdom of God' (verse 34). To be 'not far' means to be very near. Jesus perceives that the scribe, in his faith and openness, has come close to the heart of the kingdom. In this small but extraordinary scene — particularly within the wider context of conflict and entrapment — one of the enemy is actually won over to Jesus' side.

III. Jesus' counter-attack against the scribes
Mark 12, verses 35 to 44

The scribe's question is the last in the series of questions directed at Jesus. Its end result is to silence the enemy: 'After that, no-one dared to ask him any question' (verse 34). The authorities are silenced by Jesus' answers and by the spectacle of one of their own number going over to Jesus. It is now Jesus' turn to respond and he does so in two ways. First, he directs a question at the scribes that they cannot answer (verses 35 to 37) and second, he attacks them for their exploitation of the poor (verses 38 to 44).

The question that Jesus asks in verses 35 to 37 is not easy for us to understand today. The quotation is from Psalm 110, verse 1. Originally, it was a royal psalm, probably associated with the coronation of the king. On such occasions the king could be referred to as 'Lord', although strictly speaking the title belongs only to God (see Psalm 2, verse 7). The New Testament quotes this Psalm in a number of places and interprets it as pointing to Jesus as king/Messiah.[15] Here, Mark is concerned with what it means to say that Jesus is the Messiah.

At first, Jesus seems to be suggesting that the

Messiah cannot be both David's Son and also David's Lord. Is he saying that the quotation from Psalm 110, verse 1 ('The Lord says to my lord, "Sit at my right hand until I make my enemies your footstool"') is a *contradiction*? In fact, the point is an important one and contains a paradox found elsewhere in Mark's Gospel, though in somewhat different terms.

At Caeserea Philippi, for example, Peter names Jesus as the Messiah (Mark 8, verse 29), but Jesus goes on immediately to relate this to his death (verse 31). So also in chapter 12, Mark points to the way that Jesus as Messiah breaks down people's expectations. The same Jesus who is Son of David by virtue of his descent is now to be revealed as Lord of all through his death and resurrection. The Psalm is true, says Mark, but in an unexpected way. Only the events of Jesus' life and death make sense of the apparent contradiction. For Mark — as for the New Testament in general — the Easter events reveal that Jesus is Lord of all.

Having attacked the scribes' understanding of the Messiah, Jesus now turns to their behaviour, especially towards the poor. Their self-conscious religiosity, says Mark, is utterly contradicted by their behaviour and lifestyle. They 'devour widows' houses and. . . say long prayers' (verse 40). Jesus echoes the judgment of prophets such as Amos and Micah who also railed against Israel for its oppression of the poor.[16] Widows, in particular, were vulnerable to exploitation. Along with orphans, they are used in the Bible as symbols of those who are most poor and therefore most in need of the protection of the Law. As 'doctors of the Law', the conduct of the scribes is especially reprehensible.

It is in this light that the story of the 'widow's mite' must be seen (verses 41 to 44). Often we have seen it as Jesus commending the woman for her generosity which means more than the donations of the rich, because it involves real sacrifice on her part. This view does not make much sense of the story here.

Why is it commendable for a desperately poor widow to contribute to the Temple the very means of her subsistence? It would be the equivalent today of commending an unemployed person for putting the whole of their dole cheque into the collection plate in church or giving it all to charity. We do not — indeed, ought not to — expect people to give away the money they need for the bare necessities of life.

At the same time, the episode occurs in the context of conflict and counter-attack. Jesus is attacking the religious system for its hypocrisy and oppression of those who are poor.

It makes more sense to see the widow's reckless generosity as itself the sign of how she has been exploited by the scribes and the Temple system. Jesus is not so much commending her generosity —

though that is undeniable — as criticising those who have manipulated and exploited her. They have placed upon her a burden of giving which is motivated by their greed and inhumanity. According to Mark, she is the victim of those who 'devour widows' houses and . . . say long prayers' (verse 40). Deluded by their manipulation and pretence of piety, she gives up her basic means of survival.

This represents a further attack on the Temple which 'has robbed this woman of her very means of livelihood'.[17]

Conclusion

The theme of Mark 12 is conflict. On the surface, it is the conflict between Jesus and his opponents. On a deeper level, this signifies the conflict between the powers of good and evil, the new order and the old. Mark perceives clearly here that evil and oppression can exist at the centre of religion. Indeed, such oppression can flourish in religious structures and among religious people, precisely because so much can be hidden under the cloak of piety and pastoral care.

Mark is not singling out Jewish leaders more than other religious leaders, including those in the church. Nor is he saying that leadership and religious organisation are bad in themselves. The point is a broader one: the church, and Christian communities in general, need to be wary of the hypocrisy that can lurk beneath apparent sincerity and religious enthusiasm. A religious and pious exterior can conceal some of the most insidious forms of evil in human life. The forces of the old order are to be identified, not by their piety and respectability, but rather by their concrete concern for truth and justice. The openness of the scribe is an example of the kind of integrity which is open-hearted to the other. For Mark, the forces of the old order and the forces of the new order are found often in places where we might least expect them (see Mark 9, verses 38 to 41).

Mark's message in this chapter challenges us as Christians to a new way of seeing the world around us. We need to be careful of developing an 'us and them' mentality which believes that goodness and true religion are only found within our own religious community or grouping. In this day and age, we cannot be naive about ourselves as Christians, nor about the church.

A contemporary example of the way evil can hide beneath a cloak of piety is that of sexual abuse. This can and does happen both in 'good' Christian homes and in relationships between Christian leaders and those for whom they are responsible. We need to be very discerning in these matters. It does not mean we become cynical about the church or Christian community, or even our leadership. What it does mean is that our love for the church and its leaders should be neither credulous nor overly defensive.

Our primary commitment must be to God's kingdom and God's justice. Sometimes, Mark tells us, that sense of commitment may place us, as it did Jesus, over against the religious people who are more capable than most of hypocrisy and judgmentalism.

Discussion questions

Talking it through

1 What is a parable? What is the key point in the parable of the vineyard and the tenants? How does this story affect you?
Do you feel:
  sympathy?
  anger?
  fear?
  guilt?

2 Why is self-love vital to the carrying out of the second great commandment?

3 How are the first and second great commandments linked? Can you have either one without the other? Why do you think the way you do?

4 What evidence is there that in verses 42 to 44 the woman was not so much being commended as the scribes being condemned?

What important principle of Bible interpretation is being used here? How important is it?

5 Why is a religious organisation particularly prone to exploiting people? How can principles of truth and justice be brought to bear in the following situations (which actually do occur!):
(a) sexual abuse by a church leader in counselling situations?
(b) a husband with church links being physically violent towards his wife?
(c) a church leader financially exploiting a congregation?

Widening our horizons

1 What would you have done in each of the following contexts and why:
   (a) As a German in Nazi Germany, you are asked to lie to the authorities about Jews you are sheltering.
   (b) As an American opposed bitterly to a war the US is engaged in, you can know the proportion of your taxes which go to the war effort.
   (c) As a citizen in a country with compulsory voting, you disapprove of the amorality of all the candidates' platforms. To what extent do you believe we should be loyal to the state?

2 Can someone whose first loyalty is to God be a member of a political party? Can one be a candidate for parliament if the party requires total loyalty on every issue?

3 How do you react to each of the following:
   (a) The plight of not just the unemployed but the unemployable, i.e. those who for

decades/generations have not worked and have lost the motivation to do a fair day's work.

(b) The irrational hatred of opposed ethnic groups with generations of feuding behind them who, in the face of their overwhelming hatred, are powerless to speak to each other and so plunge their country into poverty and civil war.

Is there anything we or others can do to implement constructively the second commandment in such situations?

4 The widow is an important symbol of oppression in the Bible. Using Jesus' approach to powerlessness as a model, what can be done for the following oppressed groups:

(a) women and children who suffer in civil wars?

(b) tenants put out on the street as a result of higher rents which they cannot afford?

(c) a woman caught in a marriage where the husband is abusing the daughter?

3
Mark's understanding of the last things

MARK CHAPTER 13, VERSES 1 TO 37

AFTER THE CONFLICT of the last two chapters of Mark's Gospel, Jesus now turns his attention away from the authorities (silenced at Mark 12, verse 34) to the disciples and the crowds (chapter 13).[1] Mark 13 is in many ways an extraordinary and difficult chapter. It is in the form of a sermon delivered by Jesus on the Mount of Olives opposite the Temple and immediately preceding the story of his passion and death.

Right from the start it presents us with two basic problems. First, how are we to understand the unusual imagery of the chapter? It is full of dramatic and bizarre images of persecution, betrayal, earthquakes, famine, stars falling from the sky and the coming of a mysterious figure called the 'Son of Man'. It is not easy to see how Mark intends us to interpret these strange figures. The second problem is to do with Mark's overall narrative. What place does this chapter have in Mark's story? Why does it seem so out of place in the chapters dealing with Jesus' last days in Jerusalem?

If we begin with the second question, we see on closer inspection that there is a tighter link between this chapter and the chapters surrounding it than is at first apparent. Mark 13 is closely bound with what has gone before. This is particularly the case with the theme of the Temple. Most of the events which have occurred so far in Jerusalem have been focussed in some way on the Temple. Indeed, it has been the symbolic centre of the conflict between Jesus and the religious leaders. This theme is continued in chapter 13 in the opening verses.

At the same time, Mark 13 is also closely bound to the story of Jesus' passion and death (chapters 14 and 15). There are a number of important points which the two sections of the Gospel share in common. Many of the events described in Mark 13 already begin to take place in Jesus' arrest, trial and death and especially in the response of the disciples during the passion story. Moreover, Mark 13 is tied to the following chapters because it has a similar function to the farewell speeches made by dying heroes in the Old Testament. Just as Jacob, Moses and others give a long speech before their death (see Genesis 49 and Deuteronomy 32 and 33), so too Jesus makes a speech. Like them, he speaks about the future after his death. Like them, he warns, reassures and encourages the community gathered around him, preparing them for the dangers and trials when he is no longer with them.[2]

To realise how Mark 13 fits within the story of Jesus' last days, however, is only part of the problem. The other issue is the strange nature of the language and images. In fact, this language belongs to a type of literature called 'apocalyptic'. It is similar to the type of language we find in the Book of Revelation. It is also present in other places in the Gospels, some of which are direct parallels of this passage in Mark (Matthew 24 and Luke 21; see also Matthew 10, verses 16 to 42 and Luke 17, verses 20 to 37).

Jewish apocalyptic is a distinctive way of seeing the world coming out of situations of conflict and persecution. The Book of Daniel is an example of this kind of work in the Old Testament and it has had a major influence on Mark's Gospel as a whole, as well as on Mark 13 in particular (see especially Daniel 7, verses 13 and 14, and Daniel 12, verses 10 to 13). The only hope for the small suffering community in all its tribulation is seen as the intervention of God. It will mean the overcoming of the 'old age' of evil and suffering, and the beginning of God's 'new age' of peace and justice. Apocalyptic looks for the signs of the End which will indicate that the last battle has been joined and that God's triumphant kingdom is close at hand. It uses secret images and pictures that only the insiders understand. It is a kind of code language to describe the two ages.

The Christian church took over many of the ideas and language of Jewish apocalyptic and related it to their own experience and understanding of Jesus. Mark 13, for example, uses apocalyptic ideas to give expression to a hope and faith in Jesus, and also to make sense of the suffering and persecution of the community. In the apocalyptic tradition, Mark sees suffering as itself a sign of the End. The images of this chapter are concerned not so much with the dim and distant future, but with events which are already taking place in the community and are projected onto the future. In this context, Mark offers a struggling community hope and reassurance for what the future will bring.

Before exploring these issues in greater detail, we begin with a structure for the passage. One way of reading the chapter is based on the key questions which the disciples ask of Jesus in verse 4: 'Tell us, when will this be, and what will be the sign that all these things are about to be accomplished?' The rest of the chapter is Jesus' answer to the questions in reverse order:[3]

72/Mark's understanding of the last things

I. Setting: The two questions
Mark 13, verses 1 to 4
* Destruction of the Temple (verses 1 and 2)
* The question of the four disciples (verses 3 and 4)

II. 'What will be the sign?'
Mark 13, verses 5 to 23
* Signs of war, famine, earthquake: beginning of labour pains (verses 5 to 8)
* Signs of betrayal, persecution and death: witness of martyrs (verses 9 to 13)
* Signs of the 'desolating sacrilege': shortening of the days (verses 14 to 23)

III. The coming of the Son of Man
Mark 13, verses 24 to 27
* Signs in the heavens (verses 24 and 25)
* Appearing of Son of Man (verse 26)
* Gathering in of an elect community (verse 27)

IV. "When will this be?'
Mark 13, verses 28 to 37
* Parable of fig tree: note the signs (verses 28 to 31)
* Parable of the traveller: be ready at any time (verses 32 to 37)

Here we note that the central scene (the coming

of the Son of Man) is the climax of the chapter and the ultimate source of reassurance for the community. The two questions of verse 4 frame the scene on either side and provide both the lead-up to it (verses 5 to 23) and the implications of it for living in the present (verses 28 to 37).

I. Setting: The two questions
Mark 13, verses 1 to 4

Mark sets the scene carefully in the opening verses. An unnamed disciple admires the huge stones and buildings of the Temple (verse 1).[4] This reflects the typically Markan theme of misunderstanding. Despite what has occurred in the 'cleansing' of the Temple, despite Jesus' confrontation with the Temple authorities, the disciples are still in awe of the Temple and admire its external dimensions and beauty.

Jesus, however, exposes this misunderstanding in the most uncompromising terms (verse 2). Far from being an eternal symbol of true religion, the Temple is to be destroyed, says Mark, and its place taken by the new community around Jesus (see Mark 3, verses 31 to 34). Once again, we see the disciples misunderstanding Jesus' basic message.

The prophecy of the destruction of the Temple helps us to guess the dating of Mark's Gospel. The Temple was in fact destroyed by the Romans during the course of the Jewish War in AD 70. Mark was probably written either just before or just after the war and therefore the events referred to in this chapter are very much part of the author's world. Mark 13 is written in the context of this crisis and the author sees the destruction of the Temple as part of God's will and as a sign of judgment on the Temple leaders.

In the following verses, Jesus is approached by the inner group of four male disciples — the same four whom Jesus first called in chapter 1, verses 16 to 20 (Peter, James, John and Andrew). As in Mark's collection of parables (Mark 4), Jesus here gives private teaching to the disciples, which later seems to broaden out to include a wider group. The reader recalls that three of these disciples have shown an abysmal ignorance on the journey to Jerusalem: they have not understood Jesus' message of the cross at all (see Mark 8, verses 27 to 33, and Mark 10, verses 33 to 45). That, and the misunderstanding of the disciple in chapter 13, verse 1, makes us suspect that the disciples' questions in verse 4 are another example of misunderstanding. The disciples still see the kingdom in terms of power and triumph over God's enemies.

Jesus responds by directing them back to the cross: to suffering and persecution as part of the cost of following in his way. Significantly, the context for this message is the Temple, the symbol for Mark of all that is hostile to God and God's kingdom.

II. 'What will be the sign?'
Mark 13, verses 5 to 23

Jesus now begins the sermon by outlining the signs which will show that the End has come. This theme is very much part of Jewish apocalyptic: there will be a number of signs which will indicate to the community of believers that the End is near. Moreover, these signs are to consist of disasters, persecution and suffering. They represent the last attempt by the forces of evil to overpower the forces of good. Nevertheless, goodness will finally triumph and the small, suffering community will be vindicated.

These signs are called 'messianic woes'. Their effect will be apparent not just in the community, but also among the nations of the world; even nature will be affected by the signs of the End. In Mark's view, the woes are the sign that the Messiah will soon appear and God's kingdom will be finally established.

The central image in the first part of this section (verses 5 to 8) is that of childbirth, another common apocalyptic image. The woes are to be like the labour pains that are a necessary part of giving birth. Although they are, at one level, fearful and disastrous (wars, earthquakes, famines), on a deeper level they will turn out to be like labour pains. They will give birth ultimately to God's reign.

This message for Mark's struggling community

does not remove the pain of suffering, but it does offer a real sense of hope within that context. Just as in giving birth the pain sometimes reaches beyond the limits of human endurance, so with the agony of persecution. Nevertheless, it is not passive or meaningless suffering, because it is part of the active labour of birthing.

Mark also warns the community against false Messiahs and false leaders. Once again the warning reflects Mark's context. In Mark's period of crisis, many are claiming to be God's messengers. Perhaps these false leaders give a message of 'peace where there is no peace' and so lead the community astray (verses 5 and 6). Whatever their message, Mark may have specific individuals in mind, either in the wider Jewish-Christian context or within his own community.

What we need, he says, is to discern the truthfulness of any who claim leadership, any who claim to speak on behalf of God. The true word of the kingdom leads disciples to face suffering and not run away from it. In Mark's understanding, therefore, true hope lies on the other side of suffering — not by avoidance, but by awareness, wisdom and hope in the face of suffering.

Mark now turns to the way the 'woes' will affect the inner life of the community (verses 9 to 13). The disasters at the national and international level (threatened invasions and wars) and at the cosmic level (famine and earthquake) will also happen at the community level. There will be the same experience of disintegration, the same sense of basic human values breaking down. Yet these verses function to encourage as much as to warn of the dangers. The hope is that betrayal, persecution and martyrdom will all bear witness to the good news for all nations (verse 10).

Once again, this suggests the image of labour pains. What seems to be a situation of unalleviated and pointless suffering turns out to be inherently meaningful. Even the death of members of the community will be a powerful testimony to the kingdom.

Moreover, such testimony will happen because of the power of the Holy Spirit who will speak with and through the martyrs, witnessing to the truth of the gospel in the most extreme circumstances (verse 11). Similarly, the endurance which is called for will be done in the strength of the Spirit (verse 13b). These verses recall the words of Jesus in Mark 8 when he has just finished setting out, for the disciples and the crowds, the way of the cross: 'Those who are ashamed of me and of my words in this adulterous and sinful generation, of them the Son of Man will also be ashamed when he comes in the glory of his Father with the holy angels' (verse 38).

So far we have seen two basic signs of the End: the first on the international/cosmic level (wars, earthquake, famine) and the second on the level of the community (betrayal, persecution, death). The third sign is the most mysterious and most difficult to understand and it occurs in the last part of the section (verses 14 to 23). This sign is called the 'desolating sacrilege' (verse 14) and only makes sense in the light of the past history of the Jewish people.

In 168 BC, the Syrian king, Antiochus IV Epiphanes, after capturing Jerusalem and stealing the sacred vessels from the Temple, set up an altar to the Greek god Zeus and possibly a statue. The books of Maccabees tell the story and refer to the altar as the 'desolating sacrilege' (1 Maccabees 1, verse 54; 2 Maccabees 6, verse 2). The Book of Daniel also makes reference to it ('the abomination that makes desolate': Daniel 11, verse 31; 'the abomination that desolates': Daniel 12, verse 11).[5]

What does Mark have in mind by referring to this past event? And why does he speak of it as something to happen in the future? That Mark takes it seriously is emphasised by the words in parenthesis ('let the reader understand': verse 14) — the only place in Mark's Gospel where the reader is addressed directly. It is quite likely, as we have already noted, that Mark is writing in the context of the Jewish War (AD 66–73) and has in mind the destruction of the Temple by the Romans (cf. Luke 21, 20 which refers to Jerusalem being surrounded by armies). If so, Mark's cryptic language here can be explained by the political dangers of being more explicit, given the hostility of the Romans.[6]

The fact that Mark is describing the conditions of war — or at least intense persecution — is confirmed in the following verses. They vividly describe the plight of refugees forced to flee their cities and homeland (verses 15 to 19). As in the previous sub-section (verses 9 to 13), Mark begins on a note of caution and moves to encouragement and consolation. He begins by warning the community to flee and then encourages them.[7] Thus the terrible warning of the suffering which will particularly afflict women and children (verse 17) is followed by the consolation that God will shorten the days (verse 20): the suffering will not last for ever. Mark then concludes the section by repeating the warning against false Messiahs and false prophets (verses 21 and 22).

III. The coming of the Son of Man
Mark 13, verses 24 to 27

As noted earlier, verses 24 to 27 are both the centre and climax of the chapter. The warnings and instructions of the previous section (verses 5 to 23) and the following section (verses 28 to 37) frame on either side the central section of the sermon.

These verses articulate the strong sense of hope which Mark holds out to his community. The language is typically apocalyptic and dependent — like the rest of the chapter — on the Book of Daniel. The imagery describes events on a heavenly dimension, indicating the proximity of the End. Thus the section consists of three elements: cosmic events signalling the end of the age (verses 24 and 25), the coming of the 'Son of Man' which is the central statement (verse 26), and the consequences of his coming (the gathering of the believers by the angels, verse 27).

The most interesting and difficult feature of these verses is the meaning of the title 'Son of Man' in verse 26. Most likely this refers to a divine, heavenly figure sometimes referred to in Jewish apocalyptic. The origins of the phrase are probably to be found in Daniel 7, verses 13 and 14. It is worth quoting these verses in full:

> I saw in the night visions,
> and behold, with the clouds of heaven
> there came one like a son of man,
> and he came to the Ancient of Days
> and was presented before him.
> To him was given dominion
> and glory and kingdom,
> that all peoples, nations and languages
> should serve him;
> his dominion is an everlasting dominion
> which shall not pass away,
> and his kingdom one
> that shall not be destroyed (RSV).

The links between this passage and Mark's Gospel are striking. The theme of the Gospel is the kingdom of God (Mark 1, verse 15), of which Jesus is the bearer in both word and action. This, too, is a major theme of this section of Daniel. Moreover, Jesus is called 'Son of Man' at a number of points in Mark's Gospel. This in itself is strange because, although Mark uses the title fourteen times throughout the Gospel, he does so in several different ways and it is not easy to see the connection between them.

First, Jesus is called 'Son of Man' in places that refer to his earthly ministry (for example, Mark 2, verses 10 and 28). Second, Jesus is Son of Man by virtue of his suffering and death (for example, Mark 8, verse 31, chapter 9, verse 31 and chapter 10, verse 33). Third, he is Son of Man in the exalted sense we find here in Mark 13 (and also, for example, in chapter 8, verse 38 and chapter 14, verse 62, which is a quotation from Daniel 7, verse 13).[8]

It is likely that the last of these meanings for the title is the dominant one. If so, the common Christian understanding that 'Son of God' refers to Jesus' divinity and the term 'Son of Man' to his humanity is not the case. 'Son of Man' is, in fact, a very exalted way of speaking about Jesus. Mark (and the tradition behind him) has taken the apocalyptic picture of a heavenly being and related it not just to the future, but also to Jesus' life and death. The paradox is that the glorious figure of the End-time, in his very real humanity, is also the servant and the suffering, humiliated one.

Taking into account its apocalyptic background, therefore, we can see that Son of Man refers in Mark to an *exalted, divine figure*. He carries out judgment on behalf of God and will come at the end of time to judge the world.[9] The power he possesses is God's own power and he will use it to vindicate the suffering community (verse 27), which has experienced terrible persecution and yet remained faithful.

For Mark's community, this is where the real source of hope lies: in God's final intervention in human history through the final coming or *parousia* (to use the Greek word) of the Son of Man.[10]

IV. 'When will this be?'
Mark 13, verses 28 to 37

Mark now goes on to spell out the implications of Jesus' parousia. How then are we to live, knowing that Jesus is to appear and gather all things to himself? In particular, we can imagine that Mark's community was deeply concerned with the question of when the parousia would take place.

This concern may have arisen in part out of the urgency of their situation and the hope that their suffering would soon be over. But it is also a question which apocalyptic writings in general tried to answer. Indeed, we find a concern with how to calculate the End from both Jewish and Christian sources.

Mark's answer to the question of 'When?' may have been unexpected and perhaps unwelcome for the community. Wanting more specific indications of when the End will be, they receive instead a very different message. Mark's answer is in two parts, each based on a short parable or parabolic saying (verses 28 to 31, 32 to 37). The first is the parable of the fig tree whose foliage heralds the approach of summer (verse 28). Jesus implies that the leaves are already beginning to bud and that the apocalyptic events described in the rest of the sermon are already taking place. Here the answer to the question is: very soon.

The second part of the answer is given in the parable of the traveller. He leaves his household and instructs the servants to be prepared, day and night, for his return (verse 34). Mark prefixes the parable with two sayings. First, he refuses to speculate on the time of the End on the grounds that it is hidden in the mystery of God: not even Jesus himself knows the answer (verse 32). Second, Mark speaks of the necessity of vigilance (verse 33). Not knowing when means that the community is to live in a state of constant expectation and preparation. Christians are advised to remain alert and vigilant, always ready and joyful to greet the Lord when he returns (verses 35 to 37).

We noted earlier that Mark 13 has close links with the story of Jesus' passion and death (Mark 14 to 15).[11]

These links are particularly relevant to this section of the sermon. As we will see in the next part of the Gospel, the three disciples who appear in Mark 13 (Peter, James and John) respond in the next chapter in almost exactly the opposite way to Jesus' advice in Mark 13. This is especially the case at Gethsemane. Far from staying awake and keeping alert, they fall asleep. Far from being faithful and courageous under persecution, they fail and run away.

We have become familiar with this theme all through Mark's Gospel where again and again the disciples fail to understand the call to suffering and self-denial. Mark's picture of the failure of the disciples at Jesus' arrest and trial thus serves to reinforce the message of chapter 13. In the three disciples, we see a portrait of how we are *not* to act in the time of trial. We are thereby encouraged to respond differently.[12]

There is also a strong link between Mark 13 and Jesus' own conduct. Unlike many of the disciples, Jesus does not fail in the moment of crisis. The events which now take place in the passion story are themselves apocalyptic in character and have echoes of Jesus' sermon. Jesus is betrayed by one close to him and put on trial. He answers the accusations with courage and bears witness to the good news. His crucifixion leads to darkness over the land and the tearing of the Temple curtain, both apocalyptic signs. The latter in particular points to the destruction of the Temple. Jesus, in other words, lives out in reality the message he proclaims — though not, as we will see, without a struggle.

Mark, however, is doing more than just presenting Jesus as the true hero in opposition to many of his disciples. Mark also wants to show that there is, in fact, a close link between the signs of the End and Jesus' death and resurrection. In a sense, for Mark, the End-time has already begun with the events of Good Friday and Easter Sunday. Already, the battle has been joined between good and evil. Already, the new age is at hand and God's kingdom dawning.

Of course, Mark knows that the End is still to come in the future with the parousia of the Son of Man. But nevertheless he believes that already the Christian community is living within sight of the End and needs to be prepared for it in all aspects of its life.

Conclusion

How are we to interpret this difficult chapter of Mark's Gospel for ourselves today? We know that throughout church history, Christians have sometimes taken such passages very literally indeed. Even today we find people who are convinced they know when the End will be, despite what Jesus says in verse 32. Mark tells us that we can never be sure. It is possible to be overly confident about interpreting such passages in the Bible. In fact, Mark 13 does not contain a blueprint of what the future will be. We need to be careful of becoming obsessed with the question of the future and ignoring the reality of the present. To do so is to move away from Mark's intentions in presenting us with this material.

In one sense, what Mark is suggesting is that God's future is always pressing upon us, always calling us to live in hope, always challenging us to discern intelligently the signs of the times in the midst of suffering. We are not to be discouraged by suffering because, in God's hands, it can become the labour pains of the kingdom. As Eduard Schweizer puts it:

> All suffering in the present time is subject to God's sovereignty. This suffering is part of a history over which God is Lord and which he will bring to fulfilment. Thus keen anticipation and glad hope characterise the attitude of the church toward history despite all its suffering.[13]

We are to live with a sense of expectation and hope that God's kingdom will come, no matter how bad things look in the world around us. We may not know the when or the how of the End, but we do know that the reality of God's future will one day overtake and transform the present. Good will triumph over evil. The church, for all its faults and inadequacies, will be gathered with the whole of creation into the final embrace of God.

This expectation of the parousia and all its accompanying drama is no excuse for us to sit back and let the world rot. Some Christians seem to suggest this and it has given apocalyptic a bad name among many people. Hope in God's future does not mean that we no longer care about the plight and suffering of the world in the present. On the contrary, for Mark's community and for us, it means the opposite.

In every season of Advent, when we look and long for the coming of Jesus, we find a renewed call to hope and action. We are summoned to a deeper commitment to the world in its suffering and a stronger sense of the importance of our co-operation in bringing about good upon the earth, a preparation for the coming of God's kingdom.

Certainly, it does not depend on our efforts, but God does use us to bear witness to the justice, truth and goodness of the kingdom. We are called to live out of a profound sense of openness to God's future, to live in hope in a world where there is all too little hope, to commit ourselves daily to the coming of the kingdom in the world. This is the challenge of Mark 13: to live with a sense of openness to the future and, at the same time, a commitment to action in the present. Above all, it means a deepening faith in the word and promise of Jesus that his parousia will bring salvation to us and to the world.

Discussion questions

Talking it through

1 Do you think the comparison between labour pains and childbirth on the one hand, and persecution and the End on the other is an appropriate one? What does such a comparison tell us about the way God works?

2 Why is it particularly appropriate that the term 'Son of Man' be used to describe Jesus in verses 24 to 27? What apparent paradox does the term contain? Does the term add anything to your understanding and appreciation of Jesus?

3 State simply how you would describe the hope for the future, as outlined in Mark 13. How does Mark suggest we prepare ourselves for it?

4 There were some, particularly in the mid–1980s in the US, who argued that we should welcome signs of evil, such as the possibility of a nuclear holocaust, and let events take their course, because such events were signs of the End-times and to interfere is to delay. In what ways is this a *misunderstanding* of Mark 13?

Widening our horizons

1 There is no single answer to the mystery of suffering. But how can people be helped to work *through* their suffering rather than walk around it — to find that true hope in suffering lies in its awareness, not its avoidance?

What support would you give to those facing the following situations 'in extremis':
(a) the physical pain of a terminal cancer patient requiring very high dosages of morphine to be comfortable?
(b) the emotional pain of betrayal by a loved one?
(c) the spiritual pain of feeling alone in the universe, abandoned by God?

2 What can we learn about hope from each of the following 'suffering communities':
(b) the early Christian church (through their writings)?
(b) the Anabaptists of the sixteenth and seventeenth centuries (through their writings)?
(c) the Afro-American descendants of former slaves in the US (through their spirituals)?

Mark's understanding of the last things/91

(d) the persecuted branches of the Christian church in Nazi Germany (through the writings of Dietrich Bonhoeffer and others)?

(e) today's base Christian communities of Latin America (through what is written about them)?

Are there any worthwhile common threads in these experiences from which we can learn? Is there a key to turning adversity and persecution into something glorifying to God?

3 In what ways do each of the following fulfil God's purposes for the present *and* the future:
(a) helping a confused old person across a busy road?
(b) buying gifts for Christians from an Aid organisation that sells the goods of the Third World poor?
(c) giving shortterm holidays to the children of Chernobyl or some such international disaster area?
(d) spending time with a young mother with inadequate life skills to handle the demands of parenthood?

4
The lead-up to Jesus' arrest: Passover

MARK CHAPTER 14, VERSES 1 TO 31

WITH THE OPENING WORDS of Mark 14, the story of Jesus' passion and death actually begins. Mark sets everything that happens in the context of the Jewish feast of Passover (verse 1). This is important for his understanding of Jesus' death and particularly for the account of the Last Supper which Jesus shares with the disciples.[1]

For Mark, Jesus' death brings about a new agreement, or covenant, between God and human beings. This, however, is in continuity with the old covenant that God previously made with the people of Israel. The new covenant is not meant to do away with the old, but rather brings a new emphasis to God's ongoing love for human beings. Mark puts Jesus at the centre of God's love and fidelity. Through Jesus' death, God opens the covenant to all people — Jew and non-Jew — and, in doing so, overturns many of our human expectations of the way God works.

This section of Mark's Gospel is concerned, therefore, with the meaning and significance of Jesus' death. It is equally concerned with what it means to be a disciple of Jesus and to be part of the community of disciples. Above all, Mark deals with the theme of failure in discipleship by presenting Jesus' death in the context of denial, desertion and betrayal on the part of those closest to Jesus. Here, Mark is trying to say something profound to his community. It is not the heroes of faith who are invited to the Table, but rather the broken, fragile group of disciples who let Jesus down in his hour of need. As one writer has expressed it:

> Central to the whole of Mark's presentation of the disciples is. . . a dramatic and inevitable movement on their part towards failure. This failure will reach its depths in Mark 14: 50: 'And they all forsook him, and fled.' Equally central to the Markan story of disciples, however, is the never-failing presence of Jesus to his ever-failing disciples.[2]

Mark's story of Jesus' death is also set within the context of growing hostility between Jesus and the religious establishment in Jerusalem (verses 1 to 2).

Many of the leaders are challenged by the proclamation of God's kingdom. In the previous chapters (Mark 11 to 13), as we have seen, Jesus has challenged the power and authority of the old order of things. Jesus represents the power of God's new order of things, just as the leaders, in Mark's view, represent the power-seeking of the old order. It is quite clear now that they will strike back at Jesus' challenge to their power. However, they can only do so in secrecy and by stealth: Jesus' popularity among the Jewish people is too strong for them to operate openly. It is in this context of the threat to Jesus' life and the feast of Passover that the scenes in chapter 14 take place.

The structure of the passage is typically Markan. The story of the plot (**a** and **a¹**) provides a frame for the story of the anointing (**b**). At the same time, the Last Supper is a kind of parallel to the story of the anointing. Both occur in the context of a banquet and both are concerned with who Jesus is and what it means to be a disciple of Jesus. This can be set out as follows:

I. The plot to kill Jesus
Mark 14, verses 1 to 2 (**a**)

II. The anointing at Bethany
Mark 14, verses 3 to 9 (**b**)
* Unnamed woman anoints Jesus' head (verse 3)

* Negative response of those present (verses 4 to 6)
* Jesus' defence of the woman (verses 7 to 9)

III. Judas and the plot to kill Jesus
Mark 14, verses 10 to 11 (**a¹**)

IV. The Last Supper
Mark 14, verses 12 to 31 (**b¹**)
* Preparation for Passover (verses 12 to 16)
* Passover meal: Judas' betrayal (verses 17 to 21)
* Institution of Lord's Supper (verses 22 to 25)
* Jesus predicts disciples' desertion & denial (verses 26 to 31)

I. The plot to kill Jesus
Mark 14, verses 1 to 2

As we have seen, Mark begins the passion narrative with the determination of the leaders to get rid of Jesus. In fact, the plot to kill Jesus goes back to Mark 3, verse 6 where the conspiracy against Jesus begins. His whole ministry has aroused nothing but hostility and hatred from the religious leaders and this is intensified as the Gospel story progresses.

It reaches a climax, as we have seen, with Jesus' attack on the Temple and its leadership. Here, Mark presents us with a technical problem faced by the authorities: how can they organise Jesus' death when he is so popular with the crowd (verses 2 and 3)? Being a good storyteller, Mark delays the answer to this question and tells instead the story of a woman who anoints Jesus. Stealth, hatred and violence are about to be contrasted with open confession, love and perceptive understanding, before the full dimensions of the plot against Jesus are revealed.

II. The anointing at Bethany
Mark 14, verses 3 to 9

The story of the unnamed woman who anoints Jesus at Bethany is one of the most important scenes in this part of the Gospel. Indeed, many commentators believe that the full significance of this story is only now being acknowledged.[3]

Mark does not give a name to this remarkable woman, probably because he did not know it. We cannot, therefore, go behind Mark's story to guess her identity. Mark says nothing of her being a 'sinful woman', as in Luke 7, verses 36 to 50. Nor is she to be confused with Mary Magdalene, as many people in the past have done.

It is also important that we do not confuse her story with the other anointing stories in Luke (as we have seen) and in John (John 12, verses 1 to 8). The woman in Mark's story is simply one of a number of disciples in Mark's Gospel who are drawn towards the kingdom. She is one of the 'little people' of the Gospel (see also Mark 5, verses 1 to 20, 25 to 34; Mark 7, verses 24 to 30; and Mark 8, verses 22 to 26), who believe in Jesus and often show a deeper understanding than the apostles.

The story of the anointing is important also for the role that women play at a number of key points in the Gospel. Mark's story of Jesus' suffering and death is bound on either side by references to women disciples (see also Mark 15, verses 40 to 41, 47). These disciples are faithful to Jesus in his suffering and are contrasted with many of the male disciples who betray, deny or desert their Master in his hour of need. As we will see at Gethsemane, this latter group of disciples is unable to understand the necessity for Jesus' death. In contrast to them, the women remain faithful to Jesus and show a profound understanding of his death. Mark's story in chapters 14 and 15, therefore, is framed by the fidelity of women disciples.

Mark tells the story of the anointing carefully, making clear the way it is to be understood. It takes place in the context of a banquet at the house of an unknown character, Simon the leper.[4] The perfumed oil is extremely costly, worth almost a year's wages for a labourer (verse 3).

The woman's action in anointing Jesus is a lavish act of devotion and generosity, showing her love for Jesus. It contrasts sharply with the 'chief priests and the scribes' in verse 2 who are out to kill him. It also contrasts with the anger of those present (verses 4 and 5) who consider the action an extravagant waste of money. In economic terms, and even perhaps in terms of social justice, the action is unjustifiable: such money could have been better spent in caring for the poor.[5] Jesus, however, defends the woman's action (verse 6). As we shall see, he interprets what she has done in the highest of terms. He accepts it as a powerful symbol of love, compassion and insight.[6]

It is also of significance for Mark that the woman anoints Jesus' head (in contrast to Luke 7, verse 38 and John 12, verse 3, where it is Jesus' feet which are anointed). The action of anointing the head means more than devotion or love. It is also a symbol of the anointing of a king (see 1 Samuel 16, verses 1 to 13).

Later in the passion narrative, Mark will show Jesus crucified as a king. Here, as the story of Jesus' death begins, Mark points to Jesus as Messiah and king through the woman's extravagant action.[7] He is recognised as Messiah, not by the leaders of the people, nor even by his closest group of disciples, but by an unnamed woman. Like a number of other characters in Mark's Gospel, she is 'a paradoxical reminder to the community that "outsiders" often respond with far greater insight and generosity than the "insiders" oblivious to the presence of grace'.[8]

Jesus also interprets the woman's action, however, in relation to his burial (verse 8). Extraordinary as it may seem, she alone throughout these chapters of Mark's Gospel recognises and honours Jesus' impending death. Her action in anointing him points forward to the intention of other women to anoint

Jesus' body after his death (Mark 16, verse 1). It is a symbolic action, therefore, showing the need for Jesus' death. The unnamed woman recognises what other disciples have failed to perceive. She venerates Jesus for what he is about to do in giving his life as 'a ransom for many' (chapter 10, verse 45). Her action conveys, perhaps more powerfully than words, the wonder of Jesus' self-giving love in his death on the cross.

The climax of the story comes in verse 9. Here Jesus makes the astounding announcement that what she has done lies at the heart of the gospel: 'Wherever the good news is proclaimed in the whole world, what she has done will be told in remembrance of her.' Jesus commends in the highest terms what the woman has done and affirms the depth of her perceptions:

> In pouring out her gift over his head, she has in one action anointed him Messiah, proclaimed his death and resurrection, and made an act of total commitment to him as Lord.[9]

For this reason, she receives the highest accolade of any disciple in Mark's Gospel.[10] Through these words, Mark makes it clear to his readers that the death of Jesus is good news, echoing the opening words of the Gospel (Mark 1, verse 1): 'The beginning of the good news of Jesus Christ, the Son of God.'

The woman's action is part of the proclamation

of the gospel. It is a prophetic action using symbol rather than words to proclaim that Jesus' death is 'good news' for all.

III. Judas and the plot to kill Jesus
Mark 14, verses 10 to 11

Mark returns to the problem of the religious leaders in verses 1 and 2. Judas Iscariot offers them the solution they need: they have now found a way to kill Jesus 'by stealth'.

The character of Judas, one of the inner group of disciples, contrasts sharply with that of the unnamed woman. Both are connected in Mark's story to Jesus' death: the one proclaims it as good news for the world, the other brings it about through treachery and betrayal.

Here Mark uses a technique we have encountered elsewhere in the Gospel, in which one incident is framed between another (see also chapter 11, verses 12 to 21). The anointing is framed by the story of the plot to kill Jesus. The effect of this is to emphasise the two radically different responses to Jesus. It also shows how each of the characters is caught up, in some way, in the drama of Jesus' death.

IV. The Last Supper
Mark 14, verses 12 to 31

Jesus now directs his disciples to prepare for the celebration of the Passover meal (verses 12 to 16).[11]

This is the second 'supper' story in the chapter and it contrasts with the previous 'supper' story. Understanding and perception on the part of the unnamed woman are now replaced by bewilderment and imperception on the part of the twelve apostles.

The preparations for Passover are reminiscent of the triumphal entry (Mark 11, verses 1 to 6), where the disciples again follow Jesus' instructions and find everything miraculously ready. Mark makes the point here that everything which happens is in accord with the will of God. The theme of sacrifice and death as ordained by God is emphasised in verse 12 and gains new meaning in the scene that follows. Mark is clearly thinking in Old Testament terms by setting the Last Supper in the context of Passover and the establishing of the covenant (see Exodus 12, verses 1 to 28). These are important symbols for Mark, pointing the reader to the inner meaning of Jesus' death.

The first thing that happens at the Passover meal is the prediction of Judas' betrayal (verses 17 to 21). This is a poignant scene and the distress of the disciples shows the lack both of understanding and preparation on the part of the Twelve. They contrast markedly with Jesus who goes to great pains to prepare himself — and them — for what is to come. The absence of preparedness for the ordeal ahead on the part of the disciples is seen in their lack of self-knowledge (verse 19). They do not know themselves what lies before them and they have no idea what Jesus is facing.

The centre of the scene is the institution of the Lord's Supper or 'eucharist' (verses 22 to 25).[12] Once again, Mark narrates the story carefully. As we have seen, he relates it to the Passover feast and the eating of the paschal lamb. Just as the story of the Exodus is concerned with the liberation of God's people out of slavery and oppression, so the story of Jesus' death is also concerned with the liberation of God's people. It is the story of the same covenant God who frees human beings from suffering and evil, bringing about the reign of God — a reign of justice and love. The key symbols of God's intervention in human suffering are the same for the old covenant as for the new: sacrificial eating and drinking as symbols of participation and liberation.

In more general terms, the Lord's Supper is also related to Jesus' practice of table sharing.[13] This is a theme we find in Mark's Gospel as well as the other Gospels (see Mark 2, verses 15 to 17; Mark 6, verses 31 to 44; Mark 8, verses 1 to 10; Mark 14, verses 3 to 9). In the Ancient Near East, eating and drinking at table was a sacramental act in the broadest sense of the term. It provided an opportunity for hospitality and bonding in friendship, signifying intimacy and fellowship between those who ate and drank together. The radical aspect of Jesus' table sharing in the Gospels is that it extended to people who were, either for ritual or moral reasons, considered unclean. It included the poor and women in a relationship of equality and mutuality. Jesus' table sharing signified God's forgiveness and acceptance of people, regardless of their status in the eyes of the world. It is an important aspect of Mark's understanding of the Last Supper.

Mark's account of the Lord's Supper in these verses is simpler and sparser than other accounts in the New Testament (see Matthew 26, verses 26 to 29, Luke 22, verses 14 to 20, 1 Corinthians 11, verses 23 to 26; see also John 6, verses 52 to 58). The unleavened bread of Passover is transformed to become the symbol of God's salvation in the body of Jesus, broken on the cross (verse 22). The Passover wine is now the symbol of the new covenant, poured out on the cross (see Exodus 24, verse 8). The symbols of Passover are retained, but given new significance in the light of Jesus' death. By eating and drinking, Christians share in the renewal of the covenant and take into themselves the body and blood of Christ.

There are several dimensions to the eucharist in these verses and they relate to the three aspects of time: past, present and future. The Lord's Supper is a dynamic remembering of the sacrificial death of Jesus, the paschal lamb, by which the Christian community remembers the crucifixion of Jesus as a *past* event. It is a *present* sharing in the life of the one who died for us, the one who is still with us in the 'now' of our lives and who offers us his body and his blood. It has a *future* dimension in that it points to the future fulfilment of God's kingdom.[14]

Jesus makes a vow never again to drink of the wine until the final establishing of God's reign (verse 25). Ironically, God's kingdom will only be established on the cross. God will usher in the new age through Jesus' vulnerability, self-sacrifice and death rather than through power and triumphalism.

The words of Jesus in verse 25 are solemn and even tragic in tone, but they are also shot through with hope. Jesus' death — in any human terms, a disaster — turns out to be the way God chooses to work. Once again Mark emphasises the saving significance of Jesus' death. This becomes real for the believing community as it shares together in the sacrament, the body and blood of Christ. These are the saving symbols of the faith, and they are full of hope and the promise of new life. The eating and drinking of the bread and wine mean, therefore, a sharing in the final banquet of God's kingdom.

Like the Jewish Passover, the Christian eucharist is a sacramental way of making present both the past and the future.

As in the previous passage, we see once again Mark's 'sandwich' technique. The institution of the eucharist is framed on either side by the betrayal of Judas (verses 17 to 21) and the desertion of the other disciples (verses 26 to 31). Mark deliberately sets the eucharist in the context of the failure and inadequacy of Jesus' disciples. The point is that the sharing in Christ's body and blood is precisely for those who fail and whose faith is found wanting in the time of trial. The eucharist, as Mark sees it, takes us as we are with all our weaknesses and deficiencies.[15]

Earlier in the Gospel, Jesus announces: 'I have come to call not the righteous but sinners' (Mark 2, verse 17). We are called to the Lord's Table just as we are, and we are accepted and loved by Jesus with all our faults. It is here that we are given the life of Christ and, with that life, a living hope for the future. As the church of God we share not only in the sacrifice of Jesus, but also in God's future transformation of the world.

At the same time, our participation in Christ's suffering and death through the sharing of bread and wine also challenges us to 'repent and believe the good news' (Mark 1, verse 15). The Greek word for repentance is *metanoia* which, in Mark's context, means a change of both heart and lifestyle. It is not one event in the past, but rather an ongoing process throughout our lives. Through sharing as a community in the new covenant brought about by the death of Jesus, we are strengthened and encouraged in a life committed to conversion. This relates both to our lives as individuals and as a community in the church. Repentance, in the positive sense in which Mark uses it, means living more fully as the community of Christ. It means opening ourselves to change as we grow into the meaning of Jesus' passion and death.

In this sense, it is also clear that the sharing of

the bread and wine contains, for Mark, a note of judgment. It is in the context of the meal that Judas' betrayal is exposed and judgment pronounced upon him (verse 21). The note of judgment relates not just to the events of Jesus' life, but also to Mark's community. If, as we have seen, Mark's community was under threat of persecution, betrayal was something his readers knew from painful experience (see Mark 13, verse 12).

Here, it is clear that the eucharistic meal, for Mark is not simply an experience for individual Christians, but belongs primarily to the church community. The covenant is a bond made between God and the believing community, and it binds together the members of the community into a living bond of love and fidelity. Just as we re-commit ourselves to God through the sacrifice of Jesus in the sharing of his body and blood, so we re-commit ourselves to one another in community. Judgment is pronounced on the one who betrays the life of the community and causes the sheep to be scattered (verse 27).

Jesus' conversation with the disciples in verses 27 to 31 goes on to reveal the events that are to follow. The problem with the disciples is not just that they fail Jesus in the moment of crisis, but that they are also full of illusions about themselves. Peter, as the spokesperson for the Twelve, is convinced that he will follow Jesus even to death, if necessary. He does not believe Jesus' warning because he is so sure of his own power. He does not realise his own fragility and therefore his need for the power of God. As we will see in the next scene, Peter stands in stark contrast to Jesus, who is aware of his own fragility and weakness, and knows his need of God's power.

Yet, even here, in the midst of the disciples' illusions about themselves and their own capacities, the promise of the resurrection is given to them (verse 28). Finally, it is God's power in raising Jesus from the dead which will re-unite them as a community of faith and lead them to a faithful following of Jesus.

Conclusion

This section of Mark's account of Jesus' suffering presents us with four different responses to Jesus, all within the context of a 'supper'. It is worth summarising each of these in turn.

(a) *The religious authorities who, in Mark's view, are responsible for the death of Jesus.* They stand for the old order of things which God's kingdom challenges. They react with hostility and hatred, and try to eliminate the threat to their power by killing Jesus who is the bearer of God's kingdom. They represent the evil powers of the world which are ruthless in opposing God's new order of love and freedom.

The irony is, as we will see, that their attempt to destroy God's kingdom is the means by which God brings the kingdom to birth (see Mark 13, verse 8). There is a profound message here about the way God transforms evil to bring about good (cf. Romans

8, verse 28). It gives us hope in the face of evil and suffering in our world. God's power works to overcome evil, whatever form it may take. We can take heart from this: God's kingdom is brought to birth despite the destructive forces which oppose it.

(b) *Judas, one of Jesus' closest disciples, who betrays him.* Sin and evil exist within the church as well as outside it. In a small persecuted church, this is an understandable point of view: the danger of betrayal is always present, even from those we love most. In our context, however, which is very different from Mark's, it points us to the way in which sin and death can be present in our own structures and attitudes within the church. When we criticise evil in the world around us, we need to be careful of falling into judgmental and self-righteous attitudes.

Are we, as a Christian community, free from the taint of evil in our own attitudes and lifestyle? Jesus, in Mark's Gospel, is most critical of religious people. In his view, they are particularly prone to hypocrisy and self-righteousness.

(c) *The inner group of disciples who are enthusiastic in their following of Jesus, but tragically unaware of their fragility and brokenness.* The point will be made forcibly in the scene that follows. We, too, are chal- lenged to be aware of our weakness and points of vulnerability. Perhaps our leaders, like the Twelve in Mark's Gospel, are particularly prone to over-estimating their own strength. We need to become 'wounded healers': ministering to others, but also aware of our own poverty and constant need of God's healing power and grace.

All Christians need to have this kind of self-awareness in the presence of God. It is the gateway to true self-knowledge and also to the knowledge and love of God.

(d) *The nameless woman who anoints Jesus and who has a deep understanding of true discipleship.* It is significant that the model of the true disciple is an unnamed woman who is not part of the inner circle of disciples. For Mark, it is often those on the outside, the people we least expect, who teach us what it means to follow. Women, the poor and the outcasts in Mark often have a deeper understanding of Jesus because they are in contact with their need for God. Like the children earlier in the Gospel (see Mark 10, verse 15), it is the 'little people' who sometimes reveal more about God's love than the powerful 'insiders'. Jesus, in Mark's Gospel, has a special love for them.

We need to open ourselves more fully to such people and be more accepting of them. We need also to be careful not to associate power, in a simplistic way, with spiritual insight. In this story, the gospel is proclaimed not by the apostles, as we would expect, but by an unnamed woman who has a profound and intelligent understanding of Jesus' identity and the meaning of his death.

Discussion questions

Talking it through

1 What is the focus of Mark's concern in chapters 14 to 16:
  (a) the religious hierarchy (chief priests and elders) versus the twelve apostles?
  (b) male versus female disciples?
  (c) the privileged versus the disadvantaged?
  (d) the powerful versus those of profound spiritual insight?
  Justify your answer.

2 'Actions speak louder than words.' What makes the wordless gesture of the woman in Mark 14, verses 3 to 5 so powerful:
  (a) her faith?
  (b) her humility?
  (c) the financial extravagance of the gesture?

How does Jesus react (versus 6 to 9):
  (a) with embarrassment?
  (b) with warmth and gratitude?
  (c) with implied criticism?

3 Compare John's teaching about the Lord's Supper (in John 6, verses 53 to 58) with the accounts of the Lord's Supper in:
  (a) Mark 14, verses 12 to 26
  (b) Luke 22, verses 14 to 20
  (c) 1 Corinthians 11, verses 23 to 26.
  What do you think are the different points of emphasis in each?

4 Peter's boast (Mark 14, verse 29) is often described as arrogant boastfulness. Is that how you understand it, or is it more the boyish enthusiasm of someone who overestimates his staying power? What are some other common promises people make to God?
  (a) 'I'll follow you if. . .'
  (b) 'I'll believe in you if. . .'
  (c) 'If only I could go back to. . ., then I'd believe.'

Widening our horizons

1 Why are the 'little people' (page 107) given such prominence in Mark's Gospel? Were the socially insignificant perceived as any more important by the people of Mark's day than by people today?

What was Mark trying to demonstrate about Jesus' ministry? How can we consciously guard against condemning, patronising or ignoring those of a different social class or race?

2 Despite the suffering of people around him, how does Jesus justify the lavish generosity of the woman who anointed him (Mark 14, verses 6 to 8)? Can her action be used as a precedent for:
(a) buying an expensive Bible?
(b) commissioning a religious work of art?
(c) building an impressive worship centre?

3 How do you celebrate the Lord's Supper? Does the name (for example, the Eucharist, Holy Communion or Mass) affect how we break bread together? How can we recapture the meaning, as Mark understands it?

4 How can we be guilty of Judas-type betrayals today (see Mark 14, verses 18 to 21)? Think of the following examples:
(a) a white congregation near a black (or brown) town or suburb, but having no relationship with it
(b) the wealthy self-employed businessman, successful DINK (double income, no kids), or financially secure older couple who let everyone know they 'have it all'
(c) the special interest, lobby or pressure group (church, corporate, trade union or environmental) that unashamedly uses its political clout to achieve what it perceives to be 'good ends'.

What about inverse racism or class snobbery? Why are all such attitudes inappropriate in God's kingdom?

5
The agony and arrest of Jesus in Gethsemane

MARK CHAPTER 14, VERSES 32 TO 52

ALL THAT HAS HAPPENED so far in Mark's story of Jesus' suffering and death has been preparation for the moment of Jesus' arrest.[1] The plot to kill him is in place, Jesus has instituted the Lord's Supper and the astonished disciples have been informed that they will betray, deny or abandon their Lord in his moment of crisis. What we now see is the putting into effect of everything Jesus has said.

Only one element still remains: Jesus needs to prepare himself to meet his death. While Mark's primary concern in this section is with Jesus and the kingdom, he is also concerned to say something about what it means to be a disciple of Jesus. The point is clear in the two scenes of this section:

I. Jesus' prayer at Gethsemane and the response of the disciples
Mark 14, verses 32 to 42

II. Jesus' arrest
Mark 14, verses 34 to 52
* His betrayal by a disciple (verses 43 to 49)
* The flight of the other disciples (verses 50 to 52)

I. Jesus' prayer at Gethsemane
Mark 14, verses 32 to 42

Having attempted to prepare the disciples for what is to take place, giving them both warning (verse 27) and comfort (verse 28), Jesus now turns his attention to his own needs and his own preparation. As he has done on two other occasions in the Gospel (see Mark 1, verse 35 and Mark 6, verse 46), he now retreats for prayer (verse 32). On this occasion, however, he is not alone, but is accompanied by Peter, James and John.

These are the three disciples who were present at the raising of Jairus' daughter from the dead (chapter 5, verse 37), the transfiguration (chapter 9, verse 2), and the discussion concerning the signs of the End (chapter 13, verses 3 and 4). They are Jesus' intimate friends and they also witness at close quarters the power of the kingdom in Jesus' ministry.[2] Their presence with Jesus at Gethsemane is an indication to the reader that something of major importance is about to take place.

The story that now unfolds has a dramatic structure to it. The activity of Jesus is contrasted with that of the three disciples. Although Jesus' role is active while that of the disciples is passive, their reactions are a major feature of the story. The episode has three parts, with a setting and conclusion, which is worth setting out in full:

Verses 32 to 34 **Setting**
Jesus retreats for prayer (verse 32)
He takes with him Peter, James and John (verse 33a)
He reveals to them his distress (verse 34)

Verses 35 to 38 **First prayer**
Jesus withdraws and prays (verses 35 and 36)
Jesus returns and finds the disciples asleep (verses 37 and 38)

Verses 39 and 40 **Second prayer**
Jesus withdraws and prays as before (verse 39)
Jesus returns and again finds them asleep (verse 40)

Verse 41 **Third prayer** (implied)
Jesus returns a third time and

	lets them sleep (verse 41a)
	He announces the arrival
	of the 'hour' (verse 41b)
Verse 42	**Conclusion**
	Jesus announces the arrival
	of the betrayer

When we compare the setting with the conclusion, as outlined here, we see at once a remarkable difference between them. In verses 33 and 34, Jesus reveals an intense degree of distress,[3] which is first described by Mark (verse 33b) and then reiterated in Jesus' own words (verse 34a): '[he] began to be distressed and agitated. And he said to them, "I am deeply grieved, even to death . . ."'

As readers, we are completely taken aback by this level of suffering. Nothing in Jesus' previous attitude to his impending death has led us to expect this reaction. But, in contrast, by the end of the scene, we find Jesus calmly awaiting — and even going out to meet — Judas and the arresting party: 'Get up, let us be going. See, my betrayer is at hand' (verse 42).

What has happened between these two moments in the story to create such a change in Jesus? What is this scene really all about — for Jesus and for the disciples? There are three fundamental points that Mark is trying to make:

❏ *First, he emphasises the humanity of Jesus*

Mark gives more emphasis to the humanity of Jesus than any other Gospel. Nowhere is this more apparent than in the Gethsemane story. It is seen in the extent of Jesus' grief, as we have already noted (verses 33b and 34). There is no need to look for subtle theological explanations for Jesus' suffering here. It is only where we have difficulty in accepting the human Jesus that we need to look for explanations which are outside the text.

Jesus, as a human being, is overwhelmed at the thought of the horrendous suffering which lies ahead of him. He recoils with all his being at the thought of subjecting himself to so violent and painful a death:

> So far from sailing serenely through his trials like some superior being unconcerned with this world, he is almost dead with distress.[4]

Mark, however, pushes this further. Jesus expresses his feelings of distress and revulsion not only to the three disciples, but also in prayer (verses 35 to 36a). Mark emphasises the content of Jesus' prayer by describing it (verse 35) before Jesus prays it for himself (verse 36):

> [he] prayed that, if it were possible, the hour might pass from him. He said, 'Abba, Father, for you all things are possible; remove this cup from me . . .'

What is remarkable here is that Jesus' prayer seems to stand in some tension with his previous teaching in the Gospel. On the long journey to Jerusalem, for example, he has declared confidently the message of the cross as the way of the kingdom (chapter 8, verse 27 to chapter 10, verse 52). He has spoken of the challenge to be self-denying, to embrace suffering, to renounce power for the sake of the kingdom — for the sake of those who have nothing, who are poor, rejected and powerless. He has challenged James and John to renounce the desire for power, even in the kingdom, and instead to 'drink the cup' of suffering (chapter 10, verses 38 and 39).

True greatness in the kingdom, as Jesus teaches it in that section of the Gospel, is about taking up the cross, not about power-seeking. Throughout the journey Jesus knows full well that at the end of it lies the cross (chapter 8, verse 31; chapter 9, verse 31; chapter 10, verses 32 to 34); it is for him a journey to suffering and death and he accepts the journey willingly: 'the Son of Man *must* undergo great suffering . . . ' (chapter 8, verse 31).

Yet, in spite of this, we now find Jesus praying to be spared the 'hour'. Indeed, he repeats the prayer using the same words (verse 39) and, by implication, repeats it again (verse 41). Here at Gethsemane, in other words, where the cup of suffering is held out for him to drink, Jesus finds that he cannot grasp it. All his self-confidence on the journey to Jerusalem has deserted him. He is now confronted with the reality of his own message and he wavers.

There is nothing more human than this picture of the teacher who struggles painfully with his own teaching, who finds it easier to teach his message than put it into practice for himself. In theological terms, we see Jesus, the bearer of the kingdom, struggling with the very nature of the kingdom. Doing the will of God is painfully difficult for him. Like any other human being, Jesus has to struggle to discover and face his own destiny before God.

The point about Mark's concern with the humanity of Jesus can be seen more clearly by contrasting it with the other Gospels and particularly the Gospel of John. Matthew and Luke (who follow Mark) are closest to Mark in their portrayal of Gethsemane (Matthew 26, verses 26 to 36 and Luke 22, verses 39 to 46), although their presentation of Jesus' suffering is not so acute. John, however, is very different. There is no equivalent scene to Gethsemane. Instead, in John 12, verses 27 and 28b, Jesus expresses some distress, but there is no request to be spared the 'hour' of suffering:

> Now my soul is troubled. And what should I say — 'Father, save me from this hour'? No, it is for this reason that I have come to this hour. Father, glorify your name' (John 12, verses 27 and 28a).[5]

John, who stresses the divine origins of Jesus, does not present Jesus struggling to obey the will of God as Mark does. The difference between John and Mark is due, therefore, to a difference in emphasis. Each is trying to say something different, yet equally important about Jesus. It is not a question of choosing between them, but rather appreciating the unique perspective of each and the different contribution each has to make to a fuller understanding of Jesus. In some ways, the closest equivalent to Mark's portrayal of the human Jesus struggling to face the cross is found in the Letter to the Hebrews (chapter 5, verses 7 and 8):

> In the days of his flesh, Jesus offered up prayers and supplications, with loud cries and tears, to the one who was able to save him from death and he was heard because of his reverent submission. Although he was a Son, he learned obedience through what he suffered. . .

Here we see a parallel picture of suffering in the context of prayer which may well be a reference to Gethsemane. In Hebrews as well as in Mark, the human struggle of Jesus is portrayed in all its starkness.

❏ *Second, Mark exposes the inadequacy of the disciples*
The scene at Gethsemane is concerned as much with the role of the disciples as it is with that of Jesus.[6]

Indeed, Mark draws a vivid and dramatic contrast between them. The contrast begins in the previous scene (verses 27 to 31) where we find Peter and the other disciples totally sure of themselves and their own courage, in spite of the fact that Jesus predicts their denial and/or desertion. Understandably, they are horrified at the thought that they might deny or desert their Lord. Their mistake is that they have made no allowance for their human weakness. They assume they have the power to carry through their intentions. Mark does not present them as evil or wicked, but only as fragile human beings who lack self-knowledge.

The contrast Mark draws between Jesus and the disciples, however, is far from being one of weakness (disciples) versus strength (Jesus). On the contrary, both Jesus and the disciples are equally weak, equally fragile and equally vulnerable when it comes to facing the realities of suffering and death. The difference between them is more subtle that that.

Basically the disciples differ from Jesus in that they are full of illusions about their own power. Jesus, on the contrary, has no such illusion. He faces his vulnerability where the disciples deny theirs. He confronts his revulsion at the prospect of suffering and death; he knows his own fear and fragility. The disciples, on the other hand, for all their good intentions, have no such awareness.

The result is that, throughout the scene at Gethsemane, Peter, James and John are unable to wait with Jesus and support him in his suffering. They sleep while he struggles in prayer, effectively abandoned by his friends. Their sleep is a physical response to a situation of bewilderment and stress. Yet it is more than that.

In the previous chapter, Mark has spoken of the necessity for disciples to be alert to the signs of the End. Twice Jesus gives the warning to 'keep awake' (chapter 13, verses 35 and 37).[7] For Mark, Jesus' suffering and death are closely linked to the events of the End-time. The cross exemplifies the pattern of suffering leading to glory, which is to be the experience and lifestyle of the church (compare Romans 6, verses 1 to 11). The three disciples at Gethsemane do not understand this. They ignore Jesus' warnings to keep awake. Their sleep is the sleep of those who lack awareness, who do not understand the dynamics of the kingdom or the way that God works. In the terms of Mark 13, they are blind to the signs of the times.

Mark uses the contrast between Jesus and the disciples to address his community — almost certainly, a community which is suffering and possibly under threat of persecution. Jesus is a model for the community, not as a dashing hero who confronts suffering with bravado, but rather as one who is aware of his own weakness. Far from denying his suffering at Gethsemane, Jesus faces it honestly and without illusion.

While on the surface his prayer seems to contradict his earlier message about taking up the cross, on a deeper level his suffering at Gethsemane is part of that profound self-giving of which he speaks at Caesarea Philippi (Mark 8, verses 34 to 37). Jesus allows himself to be led to the point where his human resources are at an end. He is a model for disciples in Mark's community who are experiencing the same sense of being able to go no further. Mark tells his community that an honest self-awareness is essential for a deeper spirituality and an ongoing conversion of the heart.

At the same time, the disciples — here as elsewhere in Mark — are examples to be avoided. They stand for a false kind of discipleship which, having good intentions, nevertheless lacks self-knowledge and self-awareness. As in the interpretation of the parable of the sower, the disciples are like the seed thrown on rocky soil, which grows quickly but, having no root, soon withers away 'when trouble or persecution arises on account of the word' (Mark 4, verse 17).[8]

Mark warns his community against the kind of Christianity which, on the outside, appears to be full of confidence and strength, but underneath is hard and brittle, unable to deal with its own fragility. Jesus, not the disciples, is the model which Mark sets before his community. He is the one whose openness and self-awareness are to be imitated rather than the illusory self-assurance of the disciples.

❏ *Third, Mark shows the link between power, prayer and the kingdom*

There is more to the scene at Gethsemane than the contrast between self-awareness and self-delusion. If Mark's only message were the importance of knowing our human vulnerability, it would not take us very far and could hardly be called 'good news' (Mark 1, verse 1). But Mark has more to say than that.

We have already noted that something extraordinary happens to Jesus between his first and last words in this scene. What makes all the difference is Jesus' prayer. Although he is deprived of human support from his friends (and for which he returns three times), he finds divine support through his prayer.

There are two elements to Jesus' prayer. First, as we have seen, he prays for the hour to pass him by (verse 25b) and for the cup to be taken away (verse 36a). Second, he prays that God will answer his prayer not in accordance with his own desires, but rather in accordance with God's. He entertains the very real possibility that God will deny his request and prepares to submit himself to God's will. However passionate his desire to avoid suffering and death, Jesus is aware that there is a will greater than his to which he must submit. Open as he is to his own fragility, Jesus is open also to the will of God, even where (as now) it goes directly against his own will.

The function of prayer for Jesus in this scene, therefore, is a simple one. In communion with God, in openness and intimacy, Jesus calls on the divine power to enable him to do the humanly impossible. Recognising that he is at the end of his resources and has no power of his own, Jesus opens himself to God's power. Without such power, Jesus is unable to face the hour or take the cup; he cannot face death or renounce power over his own life — the power, that is, of self-preservation. Only God's power can enable him to do so.[9] As Jesus himself says on an earlier occasion in the Gospel and in relation to another demand for renunciation (that of wealth): 'For mortals it is impossible, but not for God; for God all things are possible' (Mark 10, verse 27).

Furthermore, as we will see later in Mark's story, the kind of power which enables us to take up the cross, this divine power, is precisely what the kingdom is all about. The kingdom in Mark's Gospel is about God's sovereign rule, but it always follows the path of suffering and self-giving. Mark's point is that only God can enable human beings to follow that path.

II. Jesus' arrest
Mark 14, verses 33 to 52
The second scene of this section of Mark's story is the arrest of Jesus.[10] It involves three groups of

characters, with Jesus at the centre, each of whom responds to Jesus in a different way: Judas the betrayer, the arresting party which consists of the crowd and members of the religious establishment, and the disciples of Jesus. Each group responds inappropriately to Jesus, although to varying degrees.

Judas is the worst of all.[11] His crime is treachery of the worst kind. He uses his intimacy and friendship with Jesus in order to betray him. Mark stresses the horror of his action by emphasising, at the beginning of the scene, that he is 'one of the Twelve' (verse 43) by showing how the moment of betrayal takes place with a kiss (verses 44 to 45) and by Judas' use of the title 'Rabbi' to address Jesus (verse 45). The latter two gestures serve as a means of identification for the arresting party, but they also reveal the depths of treachery to which Judas, as a friend and disciple, has sunk. He has used symbols of intimacy in the cause of violence and betrayal.

The exchange between Jesus and the second group, *the arresting party*, is brief. Jesus utters a reproach, not at being arrested, but at the secrecy and deviousness with which the arrest has taken place (verses 48 and 49a). Nevertheless, even that is part of the will of God, as Jesus' reference to the fulfilment of scripture indicates (verse 49b). However terrible these events (and Mark emphasises their terror), they are necessary for the bringing in of God's kingdom.

The role of the third group, *the disciples*, is to bring the scene to a conclusion and to reveal their inability to cope with Jesus' arrest. In the light of Gethsemane, we know that this inability is caused by the fact that they have not prepared themselves by means of prayer. So, for example, one of the bystanders (a disciple of Jesus) responds by committing an act of violence against the high priest's servant (verse 47).

Mark gives neither the identity of this disciple (unlike John 18, verse 10), nor does he narrate any healing by Jesus (unlike Luke 22, verse 51). The violence, however, has no impact on the arresting party. Its purpose, as far as Mark is concerned, is to underscore the disciples' lack of understanding. This point is reinforced in the closing verses of the scene (verses 50 to 52). The end result of the disciples' misunderstanding is that they abandon Jesus to his fate (verse 50).

Mark symbolises the disciples' flight in the story of the naked young man (verses 51 and 52). Rather than seeing this episode as Mark's autograph to the Gospel (as some have traditionally argued and for which there is no evidence in the text), it makes more sense to interpret it in terms of verse 50.

The young man's nakedness signifies his panic to get away and also represents the 'nakedness' of all the disciples, spiritually speaking, at this point in the story. The naked youth is an ironical commentary on the disciples' boasting of verse 31: those who have confidently asserted their willingness to die with Jesus abandon him at the first sign of trouble. Their self-illusions are (quite literally) stripped bare.[12]

Conclusion

This section of the passion narrative, in two scenes, thus draws a sharp contrast between the conduct of Jesus and that of his disciples in this time of crisis. The one who faces his own frailty and calls on God's power, Jesus, is the one who is finally able to face suffering and death in accordance with the will of God.

To reach this point of acceptance, however, is painful for him and at Gethsemane we witness Jesus' lonely struggle to obey the will of God and live out the reality of his own teaching. In contrast, the ones who deny their own human weakness, the disciples, who ignore Jesus' warnings and believe in their human power to face the crisis, are the very ones who disgrace themselves when the time comes.

In all of this, Mark is trying to say something about the kingdom and the way it works. Those who are vulnerable and open are more receptive both to themselves and also to God. The kingdom belongs to them because out of their poverty and weakness they cling to God. They know that God's power begins where their human resourcefulness ends. Whereas the disciples in their sleeping stand for the values of the world, Jesus in his wakefulness stands for the values of the kingdom — and, in doing so, stands with and alongside the poor.

We conclude this section with the words of a meditation on wakefulness by Leonard Cohen, which could well be the words of one of the three disciples after Gethsemane:

> Awaken me, Lord, from the dream of despair and let me describe my sin. . . Awaken me to the homeland of my heart where you are worshipped forever. Awaken me to the mercy of the breath which you breathe in me. . . What I have not said, give me the courage to say. What I have not done, give me the will to do. It is you, and you alone, who refines the heart, you alone who instructs mortals, who answers the trembling before you with wisdom.
>
> Blessed is the name of the one who keeps faith with those who sleep in the dust, who has saved me again and again. To you is the day and the conscious night, to you alone the only consecration. Bind me, intimate, bind me to your wakefulness.[13]

Discussion questions

Talking it through

1 Contrast Jesus' struggle in verses 32 to 42 with his statements in chapters 8 to 10 about suffering. What picture of Jesus does this give you? How do you respond to Jesus' struggle?

2 Do you see Jesus and the disciples as equally weak and fragile? If so, where does their difference lie? Is there any encouragement for us in this? How is it encouraging?

3 Why does Jesus rely on prayer in the Garden of Gethsemane? What affect does the prayer have on his behaviour?

4 What do Judas and the other disciples have in common in this chapter? What is the crucial difference?

Widening our horizons

1 To what extent are your words and actions one — what you say is what you do — in each of the following areas:
(a) reliance on God?
(b) truthfulness about yourself?
(c) reliability and faithfulness towards others?

How would you define the word 'integrity'?

2 How does self-awareness and self-understanding help us in each of the following situations:
(a) making a choice?
(b) providing comfort to the bereaved?
(c) giving advice to children?
(d) cultivating a friendship?

3 Have you ever changed your mind on some issue that, at the time, you believed you would never compromise on? How far have you been willing to change on the following matters:
(a) your attitude to God?

(b) your support of a particular political party?
(c) your initial summation of a person?

To what extent do you think willingness to change such strongly held viewpoints depends on a heightened self-awareness? What have such changes taught you about yourself?

4 What is a true friend? How vital are each of the following for the continuation of true friendship:
(a) the ability to keep a confidence?
(b) the knowledge that a friend has one's best interests at heart?
(c) regular attempts to keep in touch by phone or letter?

In what areas can friends fail and still be friends? In the light of your experience with human friends, is the term 'friendship with God' for you an appealing one? Explain.

6
Jesus on trial

MARK CHAPTER 14, VERSE 53 TO
CHAPTER 15, VERSE 20

WITH JESUS' ARREST AND THE FLIGHT of the disciples, the focus of the narrative shifts. We are no longer in the small, intimate world of Jesus and his disciples, watching them struggling to cope with impending disaster. Instead, we move to the harsh political world of hostility and hatred where Jesus confronts the powers of the old order and is apparently defeated by them.

This section of the narrative is in three scenes which parallel each other. Scenes 1 and 3 follow an identical pattern, as they present Jesus on trial, first before the Jewish Council and then before Pilate. The second scene has a close link with scene 1 as Mark frames the story of Jesus' trial by the story of Peter's denial ('trial'):

I. Jesus' trial before the council and high priest
Mark 14, verses 53 to 65
* Setting (verses 53 and 54)
* Hostile questioning: Jesus' affirmation (verses 55 to 62)
* Decision of guilt (verses 63 and 64)
* Physical abuse (verse 65)

II. Peter's 'trial' before the high priest's servants
Mark 14, verses 66 to 72
* Setting (verse 54)
* Hostile questioning: Peter's denial (verses 66 to 71)
* Peter's realisation of guilt (verse 72)

III. Jesus' trial before Pilate, the Roman governor
Mark 15, verses 1 to 20
* Setting (verse 1)
* Hostile questioning: Jesus' silence (verses 2 to 5)
* Decision of guilt: Jesus versus Barabbas (verses 6 to 15)
* Physical abuse (verses 16 to 20)

I. Jesus' trial before the council and high priest
Mark 14, verses 53 to 65

Jesus is taken immediately to the high priest where he is tried before the Jewish Council. Their purpose is to convict him of blasphemy under cover of the legal system, so they can have him put to death. The whole trial is, from beginning to end, a charade. Witnesses for the prosecution are brought forward (verses 56 to 59) whose testimony against Jesus is manifestly false; indeed, the testimonies actually conflict. The only charge that Mark makes explicit is a parody of Jesus' words at Mark 13, verse 2 where Jesus foretells the destruction of the Temple (verse 58).

There are several levels of irony in the trial. First, the false witnesses and those who have set them up are guilty of breaking the ninth commandment: 'You shall not bear false witness against your neighbour' (Exodus 20, verse 16). According to the commentary on this commandment at Deuteronomy 19, verses 15 to 21, the 'priests and judges who are in office' are required to ensure that false witnesses are exposed in order to protect the innocent. The Jewish leaders in Mark's narrrative are guilty of contravening and corrupting their own Jewish law. They are abusing the sacred office of judge in order to murder an innocent man.

Second, there is irony in the charge which is brought against Jesus (verse 58). While, as we have seen, it is a misquotation of Jesus' actual words, it is nevertheless true on a deeper level. It points back to the cleansing of the Temple in Mark 11, verses 15 to 19, which for Mark is really Jesus' condemnation of the Temple. Jesus *does* destroy the Temple in Mark's Gospel (see the tearing of the Temple curtain:

Mark 15, verse 38), not literally but in the sense of pronouncing judgment on it. It becomes for Mark a symbol of the old order of things. The destruction of the new Temple is probably a reference to the Markan community in whose hands the power of prayer and forgiveness is now centred (see chapter 11, verses 23 to 25; chapter 3, verses 31 to 35; chapter 10, verses 29 and 30; and chapter 12, verse 9).

The charge itself is, of course, ridiculous. Not only do the witnesses fail to agree; the words themselves — even if Jesus did say them — hardly constitute blasphemy.[1] What Mark is showing is the absurd lengths to which the authorities are prepared to go in order to achieve their ends. He is also emphasising that it is Jesus' challenge to the Temple authorities which is the real issue at stake. Mark's message here is profoundly political. Jesus has dared to criticise those in authority and is now suffering the consequences.

Verse 59 makes it clear that, so far, none of the authorities' attempts to convict Jesus has been successful. Turning to Jesus, the high priest meets at first only the silence of Jesus' contempt for the false testimonies laid against him (verses 60 and 61a). Finally, he confronts Jesus openly with the question of his identity and Jesus, unlike the false witnesses, testifies openly and honestly (verses 61b and 62).

The high priest's question is a crucial one for Mark: 'Are you the Messiah, the Son of the Blessed

One?' It is a question which Mark directs, not just at Jesus, but also at his readers. Mark challenges us to ask ourselves the question of who Jesus is and what he means for us. As Schweizer comments: 'The church is asked the question because this is the profession it makes even in the midst of persecution.'[2]

In response, Jesus quotes an important saying from Daniel 7, verse 13, part of which he has already quoted at chapter 13, verse 26. As we saw earlier, the title 'Son of Man' is a difficult one.[3] In Daniel, it refers to a divine being who is to carry out God's final judgment of the world at the end of time. Mark uses the title of Jesus in this way also, but he changes it by associating it with Jesus' suffering and death (see, for example, chapter 8, verse 31; chapter 9, verse 31; and chapter 10, verse 33), as well as his future coming. Thus, for Mark, the title refers to Jesus' future coming as the world's Saviour and judge, but it refers also to the suffering and death which Jesus has to undergo in order to bring the kingdom to birth. 'Son of Man' is a very high title which expresses the glory and majesty of Jesus, but a glory that is achieved only through suffering and death.

Senior describes 'Son of Man' in this way:

[It is] the title Mark consistently links with the sufferings of Jesus. Paradoxically, it is also the title that characterises Jesus' role as the triumphant figure who will come at the end of time to gather his elect and to bring world history to its consummation.[4]

The paradox which this title involves in Mark's Gospel is nowhere more apparent than in the scene before the high priest. Mark's Jesus makes one of the greatest claims about himself that we find in the whole of Mark's Gospel. However, the claim is made in the most humiliating of circumstances: in the midst of trumped-up charges, false witnesses and the blatant manipulation of power.

The point is emphasised by what follows. Once he has been condemned out of his own mouth, as it were, Jesus is convicted on the charge of blasphemy (verses 63 and 64). He is then subjected to mocking and physical abuse from his judges (verse 65). In order to torment him further, they call on him to prophesy as they blindfold and hit him (verse 65). This is another example of Mark's irony: as readers we know full well that 'the very acts his enemies are committing in trying, condemning, beating and spitting upon him *are* fulfilments of his prophecies'.[5] Throughout Mark's story we find the same ironical theme: Jesus' true status and dignity are revealed in the most degrading of circumstances. Indeed, it is precisely in his humiliation that Jesus' true identity is revealed.

One more point needs to be made about this scene. The picture of a formal and offical trial scene by the Jewish Council which Christians have often accepted has a number of problems associated with it. For example, Christians in the past have sometimes blamed the whole of the Jewish nation for Jesus' death and have consequently felt free to treat Jewish people in the most subhuman of ways. Some of this — perhaps the worst of it — has happened within living memory. Even to blame the Jewish people for Jesus' death is a fundamental misuse of scripture. Mark's concern here is not so much with the historical details of whether it was a fully-fledged trial. He presents a fairly simple picture of the events of Jesus' death, a picture which is dominated by his theological concerns.

In fact, it is unlikely that Jesus' trial was an official meeting of the Jewish Council. It is also unlikely that his death was provoked by the entire Jewish leadership. That some Jewish leaders were involved in plotting Jesus' death is clear. However, we do not know who these people were, nor the party they represented. One possibility that has been suggested is that certain Sadducees were involved in Jesus' death. Regardless of the number of Jewish leaders involved, however, it is clear that the Romans played a major role in Jesus' trial and death. The charge of sedition against Jesus was a Roman one — as were the verdict, the punishment and the executioners.

It follows from this that we need to be careful to avoid making simplistic and generalised statements about the Jewish people, either in the past or the present. Essentially, Jesus was killed by people in leadership, whether Jewish or Roman, whose power was threatened by his proclamation of God's kingdom.[6] There are such people in leadership in religion and politics the world over — in government and the church. Those who killed Jesus were not the Jewish people or even the Jewish leadership as a whole, but rather a number of individuals in powerful places who had no space in their lives for God's kingdom and who bitterly resented any challenge to their authority.

Indeed, as we will see in the next chapter, Mark's Gospel has a good deal to say about such people, about power itself and about the way it can be abused within institutional structures.

II. Peter's 'trial' before the high priest's servants
Mark 14, verses 66 to 72

The story of Peter's denial belongs with the story of Jesus' trial before the Council. Mark has carefully 'sandwiched' the two stories together, so that Peter's denial frames the narrative of Jesus' trial. Thus the setting for Peter's denial is given in verse 54 at the beginning of the trial narrative and continues once Jesus' trial is over.

This is a familiar storytelling technique to readers of Mark's Gospel and is an effective one. At the very moment Jesus is inside the high priest's palace being questioned by the high priest, Peter is outside being questioned by members of the high priest's household.

Mark presents the two stories in close relationship to each other for a specific reason. He is trying to draw a number of contrasts between two 'trials' of a very different nature.

First, Jesus' trial is before Jewish leaders, whereas Peter's 'trial' is before servants and ordinary bystanders. Second, those who put Jesus on trial are interested not in establishing truth but in manipulation and lies; those who question Peter simply want to know the truth about Peter's relationship to Jesus. Third, whereas Jesus speaks the truth about himself and refuses to deny his identity, Peter does exactly the opposite: he lies about himself, denies his own identity as a disciple of Jesus and even goes so far as to curse Jesus. Fourth, Jesus' courageous affirmation of his identity leads to a suffering inflicted by others (verse 65), while Peter's cowardly denial leads to suffering which is self-inflicted (verse 72).

To sum up: Jesus exemplifies the Markan principle of 'losing one's life in order to save it', while Peter represents the worldly path of clinging to life and risks losing the things which give meaning to his life (chapter 8, verse 35). Jesus is a model for disciples to follow, while Peter serves as an anti-model — an example of what Christians ought not to be like.

Once we have seen the basic contrast Mark wants to make between the two men, it is nevertheless the case that most of us as readers feel a good deal of sympathy for Peter. As Nineham points out, he acts both as a warning for readers of the Gospel, but also as an encouragement to us when we fail.[7] After all, would we necessarily behave any differently in such circumstances? Peter's penitence reinforces our sympathy. We know that he is acting against his own deepest desires, against the way he sees himself (chapter 14, verses 29 and 31a). As in Gethsemane, 'the spirit is willing, but the flesh is weak' (chapter 14, verse 38b).

In our identification with Peter and his horror and grief at his own actions, Mark has an important point to make. Unless we come into contact with God's power, unless we face our vulnerability and know our human weakness, we too will end up in the same place as Peter. Only God's power can enable us to overcome our natural tendency to save our own skins at the cost of what we believe and to be strong in our identity as disciples of Jesus, regardless of the cost. That is the lesson of Peter's denial.

III. Jesus' trial before Pilate, the Roman governor
Mark 15, verses 1 to 20

The final scene in this episode of the passion narrative is Jesus once again on trial — this time before the Roman authorities. It follows the same pattern as Jesus' trial before the Council. Jesus is dragged before Pilate, the Roman governor, by members of the Council (chapter 15, verse 1), just as earlier he was dragged before the Council itself. He is interrogated by Pilate, just as he was by the high priest. In both scenes, Mark gives careful attention to Jesus' response. Sentence is finally pronounced upon him by Pilate (verse 15), as it was by the high priest, and he is subjected to the mockery and physical abuse of his executioners (verses 16 to 20), just as he was by members of the Council. The parallels between the two scenes emphasise the powerlessness of Jesus before the civil and religious authorities of his day. Their abuse of power represents, for Mark, the values of the old order which stand under the judgment of God.

There are also significant differences between the two trial scenes. The first difference is that, for the Romans, the question is focussed more on whether or not Jesus is claiming to be 'the king of the Jews' (verses 2, 9, 12 and 18; see also verse 26) rather than on theological issues to do with the Temple or blasphemy. This represents an understandable anxiety on the part of Pilate who exists, after all, to protect Roman imperial interests and to quash any signs of sedition among Rome's subject peoples.

The question of Jesus' kingship bristles with *political* implications. At the same time — indeed fundamentally — the kingship of Jesus is of great *theological* significance for Mark. Through this and the following episode, Mark presents Jesus as, in truth, a king — even though his kingship is revealed in mocking, humiliation and death.[8]

The point is made most forcibly in the final verses of the scene where Jesus undergoes the mockery of the Roman guards. They mock him precisely as a king, dressing him in kingly robes, placing a crown on his head, greeting him with a royal greeting and kneeling before him (verses 17 to 19). In every sense, their purpose is to belittle and torment him, playing cruelly on the charge of sedition on which he has been condemned.

Nevertheless, this is Markan irony at its best. The scene reveals most truly Jesus' identity as king. While on the surface, the soldiers do not for a moment take seriously what they are doing, for Mark and for his readers everything they do is ironically true. Jesus is a king and the more his kingship is mocked and denied, the more it is revealed to the eyes of faith.

A second difference is that, unlike his first trial, Jesus before Pilate is even more conspicuously silent; he barely utters a single word throughout the entire scene (verse 5; see also Isaiah 53, verse 7). Once again, as in the first trial, Jesus' silence is an eloquent expression of his contempt for the manipulation and politicking that is going on all around him. It emphasises also his powerlessness in the face of the violence of his enemies. It reveals his determination — though not, as we saw at Gethsemane, without struggle — to submit in obedience to the necessity that God has laid upon him (see chapter 8, verse 31).

A third difference between the two trials is that while the centre of the first trial scene is the interrogation, the main point of the second trial scene — as a result of Jesus' silence — is very different. Instead, we see the unedifying wrangle between the Jewish and Roman authorities over Jesus, 'king of the Jews', and Barabbas, a Jewish terrorist (verses 6 to 15). Pilate's role may seem at first to be that of the willing but weak champion of Jesus. However, it is more likely that Pilate's support of Jesus, as opposed to Barabbas, is an attempt to aggravate the Jewish leaders.

If this is the case, Mark is again presenting Jesus as the powerless object of judicial manipulation and political game-playing. He is caught between two opposing, but equally corrupt, powers. Pilate's only desire all along, Mark tells us, has been to placate the crowd. Not for a moment has he believed in Jesus' innocence: 'Mark's Pilate fully understands the political character of Jesus' practice as a threat, approves of his elimination, and is willing to exchange a known political terrorist (Barabbas) in order to secure it.'[9] Finally, the choice is made: ironically, the terrorist is freed, while the healer and life-giver is condemned to death (verse 15).

Jesus is handed over to be flogged and crucified.[10]

Conclusion

The three scenes that make up this episode are perhaps the most cheerless and cynical of all Mark's passion narrative. Mark presents the leadership of the day, whether political or religious, as corrupt and corrupting. In the midst of power games and violence carried out in the name of the Law, Jesus stands as the powerless and innocent victim of injustice. Both he and Peter are mere pawns in the political manoevres of the power-brokers.

And yet both react in opposing ways. While Jesus faces the hatred and violence of his enemies with courage, Peter lies outright in order to save his skin. The one affirms his identity in the face of terrifying opposition, while the other denies it.

However, the contrast for Mark lies not in the fundamental humanity of Jesus and Peter. Both are fully human. The difference is that Jesus' reliance is on the power of God, whereas Peter trusts recklessly in his own courage. Jesus epitomises the power of the gospel which comes from God alone, which endures suffering and identifies itself with those who suffer.

Peter stands for human weakness which lacks self-knowledge and knowledge of the power of prayer. Peter's suffering is self-inflicted. It is nothing compared to that of Jesus and achieves nothing for anyone. Jesus' suffering is God-ordained and achieves everything on behalf of human beings.

It is to Jesus' suffering that the whole of Mark's Gospel points. This will be the theme of the next chapter.

Discussion questions

Talking it through

1 What actions of the Jewish authorities in the trial before the Council and high priest demonstrate that Jesus is the 'Son of Man'? What does the term mean? How does the use of this term show that in the world, good and evil, triumph and suffering are intertwined?

2 Why are the Jewish authorities, in Mark's narrative, so opposed to Jesus? Is Jesus implacably opposed to them or to what they represent? What do they represent?

3 What is the key point that is being made to us in the contrast between Jesus' trial and Peter's 'trial'? Why do we have so much sympathy for Peter, even though he has erred?

4 How sympathetically does Pilate view Jesus? What difference does the wrangling between Pilate and the Jews make to Jesus?

Widening our horizons

1 Show how the desire for power can poison those pursuing the following goals:
   (a) the leadership of a political party
   (b) marriage to a person of social prominance
   (c) the desire for success in business
   (d) the acquiring of a position of real influence in the church.

   Real or hypothetical examples might help. How can self-awareness help us cope with the problems of power?

2 How would you feel if you were each of the following and how would you act in their position:
   (a) an Anabaptist of the sixteenth century about to be killed for his belief in adult rather than infant baptism?
   (b) a person wrongly accused of unfaithfulness by a thoroughly convinced spouse (where no amount of reason will work)?
   (c) a young student ridiculed by his or her peers for holding to a literalist view of the scriptures?

(d) an honest director of a company who acts as the 'fall guy' for his corrupt colleagues?

Does Jesus' example of meek acceptance in his trial apply to such situations? Should we bear such suffering or injustice passively, or should we fight to clear our good name/vindicate ourselves? (Be *truthful* about the way you would respond!)

7
The death of Jesus

MARK CHAPTER 15, VERSES 21 TO 47

WITH THE STORY OF JESUS' crucifixion, death and burial, we reach the most important scene in the Gospel of Mark. This is the climax of the Gospel and the point towards which everything has been leading right from the beginning. Here we find the centre of Mark's theology.

Already in the Gospel, we have seen the importance of the cross for being a disciple of Jesus (see chapter 8, verse 34). Now Mark interprets the meaning of the cross in terms of God's relationship with the world. Through this historical event, Mark tells us, everything is different. We see more clearly what is already present in the Old Testament scriptures: that God is intimately involved in the world and committed to the suffering of human beings.

The death of Jesus

Through Jesus' sacrifice on the cross, the world is reconciled to God.

The episode falls into three scenes, each containing six actions or events under the headings of Jesus' crucifixion, death and burial:

I. Jesus' crucifixion
Mark 15, verses 21 to 32
* Soldiers compel Simon of Cyrene to carry the cross (verses 21 and 22)
* Soldiers offer Jesus wine (verse 23)
* Soldiers crucify him at the third hour and divide his garments (verses 24 and 25)
* Inscription on the cross: 'the king of the Jews' (verse 26)
* Two thieves are crucified with Jesus (verse 27)
* Jesus is mocked by all (verses 28 to 32)

II. Jesus' death
Mark 15, verses 33 to 39
* Darkness falls from the sixth to the ninth hour (verse 33)
* Jesus' cry of despair to God (verse 34)
* Bystanders think he calls Elijah and offer him vinegar (verses 35 and 36)
* Jesus dies with a loud cry (verse 37)
* Temple curtain tears in two (verse 38)
* Centurion confesses Jesus as 'Son of God' (verse 39)

III. Jesus' burial
Mark 15, verses 40 to 47
* Women disciples watch from a distance
  (verses 40 and 41) **a**
* Joseph of Arimathaea asks Pilate for Jesus'
  body (verses 42 and 43) **b**
* Pilate is amazed at Jesus' death and
  questions the centurion (verses 44 and 45a) **c**
* Pilate gives the body of Jesus to Joseph
  (verse 45b) **c¹**
* Joseph buries Jesus in a cave (verse 46) **b¹**
* Two of the women disciples observe the place of
  burial (verse 47) **a¹**

I. Jesus' crucifixion
Mark 15, verses 21 to 32

Throughout the first scene, Mark portrays Jesus as powerless. He is entirely in the hands of others. Moreover, he is so weak from being beaten that he cannot carry his own cross (verse 21). Even that must be done for him by a stranger, a passer-by, whom Mark names as Simon of Cyrene (clearly the two sons, Alexander and Rufus, are known to the Markan community and may even have been members of it).

Simon does not carry the whole cross, but rather the crossbeam,[1] as was the custom with Roman crucifixions.[2] The practice was an attempt to humiliate and mock the condemned man even further, though the fact that Jesus has not the bodily strength to carry it only underscores his humiliation.

There is only one active thing which Jesus does in the scene and that is his refusal to drink the 'wine mixed with myrrh' (verse 23) — probably a narcotic.[3] Mark offers no explanation of why Jesus refuses to take it. Mark's whole account of Jesus' crucifixion is similarly understated, not dwelling on the physical horror of what is taking place. However, Jesus' refusal probably reflects his determination to 'take the cup of suffering' which the Father has given him (chapter 8, verse 31; chapter 10, verse 38; and chapter 14, verse 36). It is a hint to the reader that, even in his weakness and powerlessness, Jesus is carrying out the will of God.

The whole of the scene is pervaded with mockery from start to finish. Jesus is stripped of his clothing and crucified, while his executioners gamble for his garments (verses 24 and 25). The inscription on the cross ('The King of the Jews': verse 26) is another attempt to mock and humiliate him. Crucifying him with two bandits on either side of him (they are actually terrorists) has the same effect (verse 27). His situation could not be more humiliating. Everything that happens underscores the mockery and degradation.

In this context of the casting of lots for Jesus' clothing, Mark quotes Psalm 22, verse 18. The whole psalm has had a powerful influence on Mark's understanding of Jesus' passion and death. It is a psalm of lament, the song of a righteous person crying out to God for help. Although the original setting of the psalm is a fairly general one, Mark sees it as pointing especially to Jesus. He is the truly innocent sufferer who cries out to God, and the events of his passion mirror those of the psalm. Quite apart from the reference to the dividing of Jesus' clothing, Mark is also influenced by other aspects of the psalm. Like the psalmist, Jesus is surrounded by evil people seeking his destruction (Psalm 22, verses 12 to 13 and 16). They mock and despise him (Psalm 22, verses 6, 7 and 17). They taunt him with his faith in a God who has to all intents and purposes abandoned him (Psalm 22, verse 8; cf. Mark 15, verses 29 to 31).

Quite apart from Mark's theme of the fulfilment of prophecy, the taunts of the bystanders play an important role here (verses 29 to 31). Once again we are dealing with irony, as with so much of the mocking throughout Mark's passion story. On a deeper level, these taunts contain a sublime truth. For example, Jesus' death will mean, in a symbolic sense, the destruction and re-building of the Temple (verse 29). And in verse 31, the taunt of the chief priests and scribes captures perfectly the dynamic of Jesus' ministry: 'He saved others; he cannot save himself.'

Jesus has used his power, Mark tells us, not to save his own life, but for the sake of others — those whom he has touched throughout his ministry. That is why he cannot now come down from the cross;

he remains there in order to save others. There is also a poignant touch at the end of all the derision and taunting: even his fellow criminals begin to mock him (verse 32).[4]

II. Jesus' death
Mark 15, verses 33 to 39

The death of Jesus is the central episode of this scene and by far the most significant for Mark's understanding. Mark notes the hours, breaking the day into three blocks of time: the third hour of crucifixion (verse 25), the sixth hour of darkness (verse 33) and the ninth hour of death (verses 34 and 37). The sudden fall of darkness with which the scene begins has the effect of cutting off abruptly the taunts and mockery of the bystanders. A solemn and dreadful silence now broods over everything, broken only by the cry of Jesus at the ninth hour (verse 34).

The darkness is an evocative symbol in the narrative. It has strong apocalyptic overtones, suggesting the final battle before the End: the final conflict between good and evil in which, after great suffering, God will finally triumph. It suggests also the darkness of God's judgment (see Amos 8, verses 9 and 10). The darkness symbolises also the horror of evil which Jesus undergoes. It expresses the terrible silence of God whose Son hangs crucified on the cross, rejected by the powers of the world.

Jesus' cry in verse 34 dispels the darkness and

signals that the end is near. Once again, Mark goes back to Psalm 22 to interpret Jesus' death. This time it is the opening words of the psalm, expressing the despair of the sufferer who feels abandoned by God. Mark gives the words in Aramaic (Jesus' mother tongue) and then translates them into Greek, giving strong emphasis to Jesus' last words.

Christians have not found Jesus' words in Mark's Gospel particularly easy to understand. They contradict too many of our notions of Jesus who is more divine than human and who dies — or at least ought to die — in a calm and heroic spirit, trusting in God to the end (as Luke presents it: see Luke 23, verse 46). Because Christians have found it difficult to deal with these terrible words, they have tried to tone them down. One favourite argument has been to say that Jesus is only quoting the first words of the psalm, but what he really wants to say is the whole psalm. And, since the psalm ends on a note of trust and confidence (Psalm 22, verses 22b to 31), Jesus is really echoing that trust in God's redemption.

To interpret Jesus' words like this, however, is to deny the reality of his suffering (not to mention that of the psalmist). Mark intends us to take these words quite literally: 'Jesus dies as a man torn with anguish and immersed under a tide of separation from God.'[5] Of course for Mark, Jesus does not die an atheist, nor does he abandon faith in God. Nevertheless, he dies with a sense of being abandoned by God and a cry of despair on his lips. As Mark tells the story, he is abandoned by almost everyone. His death is so stark and lonely that he even feels himself abandoned by his Father.

It is worth quoting Lighfoot's comments at this point:

> [Mark] is at particular pains to dwell upon the steadily increasing and finally complete dereliction of the Lord. The chief priests plot; one of the twelve plays into their hands and delivers up his Master; the rest of the disciples desert and their leader Peter disowns; the council of the nation condemns the Son of Man himself and he is delivered to the Gentile power; finally, the sense of his Father's presence is withdrawn. . . He who . . . in the fullness of his power diffuses health and light and life is here seen in uttermost abandonment.[6]

Meanwhile, Jesus' words create a degree of misunderstanding among the circle of bystanders. So far are they from understanding what is really going on that they fail to recognise Jesus' allusion to Psalm 22. They mistake the word 'Eloi' (meaning 'my God') for 'Elijah' and use the opportunity to taunt Jesus yet again with his powerlessness (verse 36). At this point, with another loud and agonising cry, Jesus dies.

Jesus' death is followed immediately by the tearing of the curtain in the Temple (verse 38) — probably the veil which separates the inner part of the Temple from the 'Holy of Holies'. For Mark, this extraordinary event has a double symbolism. On the one hand, it points forward to the destruction of the Temple which, in Mark's view, represents God's judgment on the old order (see chapter 11, verses 12 to 21; chapter 13, verse 2, and chapter 14, verse 58) — that same order of things which has put Jesus to death. It signifies judgment, therefore, and the end of the Temple cult.[7]

On the other hand, it has a more positive meaning. There are only two places in Mark's Gospel where the word 'torn' is used — here and at chapter 1, verse 10, where the Spirit descends on Jesus. In both passages, Mark is speaking of the tearing open of barriers which have previously been closed. Just as at the baptism of Jesus the barrier between heaven and earth is torn in the descent of the Spirit, so now at the death of Jesus the barrier between heaven and earth is definitively torn down.[8] This includes the barriers between Jew and Gentile (cf. Ephesians 2, verses 14 to 15).[9]

The centurion's confession in verse 39 is of crucial importance for this scene. There are three extraordinary features of this confession. First, these are the words of a Gentile and moreover one of Jesus' executioners.[10] It is this unexpected person who makes the central confession of the scene.

Second, this is the only place in Mark's Gospel where a human being affirms Jesus as God's Son.

Only the voice from heaven at Jesus' baptism and transfiguration, and the demons, have referred to Jesus in these terms (see chapter 1, verse 11; chapter 5, verse 7; and chapter 9, verse 7). Now at last a human being has realised what Mark's Gospel is all about; it is 'the good news of Jesus Christ, the Son of God' (chapter 1, verse 1). In every sense, the confession is the climax of the Gospel.

However, there is a third dimension to the centurion's confession. The centurion recognises Jesus as God's Son precisely in the way that Jesus dies.[11] Yet Jesus, as we saw at verse 33, dies with a cry of dereliction on his lips, believing that God has abandoned him. What is there in this painful and tragic death to draw forth a confession of faith from a Roman centurion?

The answer to this question brings us to the heart of Mark's Gospel. Mark leaves us with two statements which seem to contradict each other: Jesus dies feeling 'God-forsaken'; the centurion recognises Jesus as the Son of God. This can be put more simply. Jesus dies experiencing the absence of God, while the centurion recognises in that death the presence of God.

The cross, in other words, is a symbol for Mark of both the *presence* and the *absence* of God. The cross means by definition the absence of God. It stands for suffering, torture, humiliation, death, despair; even — to use Paul's language — curse

(Galatians 3, verse 13). Jesus is cast out of the holy city, outside the place where God dwells. In Moltmann's words: '[He] incited the devout against him and was cast out into the godlessness of Golgotha.'[12] Jesus stands in the place of suffering and death where so many human beings stand, the place where God would seem to be most radically absent.

The centurion's recognition of God's presence means that, for Mark, God in Jesus has entered into the place of human darkness and suffering.[13] God is radically present in those places and conditions that speak most powerfully and tragically of God's absence. Through Jesus' suffering, God identifies with human suffering and becomes one with us.

That is the meaning of salvation as Mark understands it. That is what the centurion recognises and what we as readers of the Gospel are called to recognise also: the presence of God in those places where God is manifestly absent.

III. Jesus' burial
Mark 15, verses 40 to 47

The last scene begins and ends with reference to the presence of women disciples (verses 40 and 47). In verse 40, Mark names three of these women — Mary Magdalene, Mary the mother of James the younger and Joses, and Salome — and speaks also of the presence of 'many other women'. The language used to describe these women is the technical language of *discipleship* ('these used to follow him') and *ministry* ('and provided for him': the Greek says, 'ministered to him'). Although Mark has not specifically mentioned these women earlier, they have been present on the journey from Galilee to Jerusalem. Their faithfulness in following Jesus to the cross contrasts with the Twelve who are nowhere in sight. The women reveal what it means to follow Jesus even to the cross.

Two of these women, Mary Magdalene and the other Mary, remain at the site until after the burial of Jesus (verse 47), taking faithfulness even further. Despite the danger, they are anxious to know where Jesus has been buried in order to honour his body with spices for burial (chapter 16, verse 1), even though it is the body of a condemned man. The two women show not only the faithfulness called for in disciples, but also the intelligent watchfulness that is required of discipleship (see chapter 13, verses 33 to 37). Whereas the three male disciples fall asleep at Gethsemane through Jesus' anguish and fail to watch (chapter 14, verses 37 to 38, verses 40 to 41), the two women disciples keep watch through Jesus' death and burial. Their Christian vigilance and their service to Jesus (cf. verse 41) is rewarded: they discover the place where their Lord is buried and are given the message of the resurrection.[14]

Just as the references to the women and the Twelve parallel each other in this scene (verses 40, 41 and 47), so too do the references to Joseph of

Arimathaea (verses 42, 43 and 46) and to Pilate (verses 44, 45a and 45b). The presence of Joseph is something of a surprise for the reader. Mark's picture of the leaders is overwhelmingly negative. All through the trial and crucifixion scenes they have been implacably hostile to Jesus. Now we find one of their number ('a respected member of the Council') who is also a disciple of Jesus.

In many ways Joseph is like the scribe of Mark 12, verses 28 to 34 who is won over by Jesus' teaching. Both men belong to the old order, but commit themselves to the new. Both do so with considerable danger to themselves: the scribe in being outspoken in his commendation of Jesus (chapter 12, verses 32 to 33) and Joseph in asking for the body of a condemned criminal (chapter 15, verse 43). Like the women disciples, he also acts in contrast to the Twelve. His courage ('boldly' verse 43: the Greek says, *'taking courage* he went to Pilate') contrasts starkly with the cowardice of the other disciples.

Pilate's role in these verses is a minor one. His surprise at Jesus' premature death (death by crucifixion could sometimes take days) emphasises for Mark the divine will that lies behind this event. Jesus dies in God's own time and not just at human initiative. Pilate's role is also to stress that, despite the relatively short time of suffering, Jesus is genuinely dead.

Matthew speaks of rumours suggesting that Jesus

was not really dead at his burial (Matthew 28, verses 11 to 15). In these verses, then, Mark is carefully setting the scene for the empty tomb and the resurrection: Jesus is genuinely dead; he has been buried with dignity and not like a criminal; two of the women disciples know where he has been buried; and they are preparing to visit his tomb.

Conclusion

Mark now comes to the end of the central scene of his Gospel. We have reached the heart of his theology in Jesus' death. God enters the arena of human mortality and poverty, identifies with it and transforms it through Jesus' sacrificial death. Mark presents Jesus on the cross as the victim of unjust suffering (a point emphasised even more strongly in Luke's Gospel, cf. Luke 23, verse 47), who is utterly powerless before the rage and hostility of his enemies. He is abandoned by almost everyone and dies feeling that even God has abandoned him.

Yet in this despair and suffering, Mark detects the hand of God. In some mysterious way, God is present in these appalling events. Although everything that happens denies the presence of God, in reality God's presence manifests itself mysteriously. Mark's theology is fundamentally about the miracle of God's presence on the cross. In Bonhoeffer's famous words: 'God lets himself be pushed out of the world on to the cross. He is weak and powerless in the world and that is precisely the way, the only way, in which he is with us and helps us.'[15] The God of the cross is the God who is found in those people and places where we would least expect to find God: in suffering, poverty, humiliation and death. Through this suffering, the kingdom is brought into being. To use the imagery of chapter 13, verse 8, Jesus' sufferings are the labour pains that bring to birth God's kingdom.

Mark presents two basic groups of people in this scene. They represent two possible reactions to God's kingdom as it is realised in the suffering and death of Jesus. On the one hand, there is the derision of the religious authorities and the sheer indifference of the Roman executioners. These stand for the old order which causes enormous human suffering and which is, at best, indifferent to it.

On the other hand, there is the presence of discipleship in places where Mark's readers would expect it least. It is found not among the Twelve — Jesus' closest companions and followers in Mark's Gospel — but among a large group of women disciples who have been present all along. It is found in the Roman centurion who unexpectedly makes the highest Christian confession of the Gospel. It is found within the Jewish Council, in the faith and courage of Joseph of Arimathaea who is prepared to stake status and reputation in order to bury Jesus with dignity.

The poet Bruce Dawe, describing the crucifixion through the eyes of the Roman centurion, concludes by describing the spectators:

> Then we hauled on the ropes
> and he rose in the hot air
> like a diver just leaving the springboard,
> arms spread
> so it seemed
> over the whole damned creation
> over the big men who must have had it in
> for him
> and the curious ones who'll watch anything if it's free
> with only the usual women caring anywhere
> and a blind man in tears.[16]

Mark's message in this story is that every aspect of our lives finds its meaning in relation to the Crucified One. When we face the picture of this man hanging dead on a cross, symbol of suffering and despair, we confront both the love of God and our own selves. In his suffering, we see mirrored our own suffering; in his despair, our despair. Yet his suffering for us and for those who are poor and vulnerable is finally what gives meaning to our lives: 'Only the willingness to accept our broken hopes and let ourselves die with that man can make full and final sense of our lives.'[17]

Above all, in the cross we see the presence of God and find the only source of hope for ourselves and for the world — for its (and our) brokenness, poverty and pain.

Discussion questions

Talking it through

1 What evidence is there in this chapter that God is intimately involved in the affairs of the world? What contribution can the events of this chapter make to our answering the question: 'Why does God allow good people to suffer?'

2 What is the significance of Jesus' last words in Mark (verse 34)? What popular notion do such words contradict? What do these words tell us about Jesus?

3 What indications are there in this chapter that Jesus' death was no ordinary death? What was particularly momentous about Jesus' death?

4 Which particular people is Mark exhorting his readers (including us) to emulate? What worthy characteristics do each of them have?

5 How can we 'die with Christ'?

Widening our horizons

1 How are the biographies of the life and death — particularly the death — of many Christian martyrs and heroes different from the account of Jesus' suffering and death here? Which do you feel more in touch with? Why?

2 'In the abyss, there is God.' What hope could be presented, based on Mark's account of Jesus' death, to each of the following:
(a) the person on the brink of suicide?
(b) the person suffering agonising pain?
(c) the person despairing because of his or her newly recognised evil?

3 Paul and the other Gospel writers shed some more light on the reason for Jesus' death (Romans 5, verses 6 to 8; 2 Corinthians 5, verse 15; John 1, verse 29), but finally there is a great deal of mystery in it.

Is mystery hard for you to handle? Does it undermine or enhance your appreciation of God? How important is it to you to push back the veil of mystery as far as possible?

8
The resurrection of Jesus

MARK CHAPTER 16, VERSES 1 TO 8

BY THE END OF CHAPTER 15, Mark has set everything in place for the events of Easter morning. Jesus is dead and buried and two of the women disciples present at the crucifixion have observed the place of his burial.

The reference to the women disciples in scene 3 of the previous episode (chapter 15, verses 40, 41 and 47) acts as something of a bridge to the next scene. While the passion narrative has focussed mainly on the men disciples (and in particular the Twelve), the resurrection narrative has its focus on the women disciples. Readers will remember that the passion narrative began with an unnamed woman disciple anointing Jesus for burial (chapter 14, verses 3 to 9). The passion narrative ends with the action of women disciples, connected in a similar fashion to Jesus' death and burial.

The structure of Mark 16, verses 1 to 8 is a simple one. The scene is bounded on either side by the arrival and departure of the women (the two at chapter 15, verse 47 has increased to include Salome). They are at first anxious over the problem of the stone blocking the entrance to the tomb. Instead, they are confronted with the stone miraculously rolled away and the young man who addresses them — clearly an angel.

Here is the simple structure:

I. The story of the empty tomb
Mark 16, verses 1 to 7

* Their purpose is to anoint the body with spices (verse 1)
* They arrive at the tomb at dawn on Easter Sunday (verse 2)
* They are worried about how to roll away the stone (verse 3)
* They find it already rolled away, huge though it is (verse 4)
* Inside the tomb, they are terrified to see a young man in white seated there (verse 5)
* He reassures them and informs them that Jesus is risen (verse 6)
* He gives them the message of the resurrection to take back to the disciples (verse 7)

II. Fear and flight
Mark 16, verse 8
* They run away from the tomb in terror (verse 8a)
* They do not tell the message out of fear (verse 8b)

The problem of the ending
Before going on to discuss chapter 16, we need to note briefly the textual problem with the ending of Mark's Gospel. In the oldest and best manuscripts, the Gospel of Mark ends at chapter 16, verse 8. Some time later, two endings were added: a shorter one and a longer one (verses 9 to 20).

These alternative endings were not written by Mark and are not an authentic part of the Gospel. Most of our Bibles include them in square brackets to show that they do not really belong, although they are certainly very old. That is one part of the problem and it is easily resolved: the two endings were added by the later church in order to round off the Gospel. They ought not to be read as part of the text of Mark.

The second problem is more difficult. Verse 8 of chapter 16 ends in a very abrupt way: 'and they [the women disciples] said nothing to anyone, for they were afraid'. There are several problems with this:

1. Mark gives no account of Jesus' appearance to the disciples, even though both Jesus (chapter 14, verse 28) and the angel (chapter 16, verse 7)

promise to meet with Peter and the others in Galilee after the resurrection.
2. If the women disciples tell no-one the news of the resurrection (chapter 16, verses 7 and 8), how does the message become known?
3. The women's fear is hard to understand and requires further explanation. It also needs to be overcome.
4. The other Gospels record stories of the risen Christ's appearances to his disciples (see Matthew 28, Luke 24, John 20 and 21). In Matthew and John 21, these appearances take place in Galilee.
5. Mark 16, verse 8 is not only an abrupt way to end a story; it is also abrupt in its grammar — the last word is very weak. The Greek says something like: 'for they were afraid, you see'.[1] It seems to stop in mid-sentence.[2]

These problems explain why Mark's Gospel was given an added ending. Early scribes saw the same problem and decided that Mark's true ending had been lost. They tried to solve it by including endings which they found elsewhere. Some modern scholars have come to the same conclusion as these early scribes: at a very early stage, soon after the Gospel was written, an accident happened to the manuscript and the ending was lost.[3] The trouble with this view is that copies of the original manuscript would have been made very soon after it was written. How could the ending be lost in every copy? An alternative explanation is that the final author of the Gospel died before completing the manuscript. In that case, why did not one of Mark's disciples finish it in his master's style? This would have presented no problem in the ancient world.

The theory of a lost ending is thus clearly a difficult one. It is highly speculative and creates as many problems as it solves.

The other possibility which is becoming more and more popular is that chapter 16, verse 8 is the true ending of the Gospel. What would happen if we took the oldest and best manuscripts of Mark at their face-value and assumed, with them, that the Gospel did in fact end on the abrupt note of verse 8? What if it was intended to end there? How then might we explain the five problems outlined above?

1. Mark gives the basic message of the resurrection (verses 6 and 7) and may not have felt the need to tell the rest of the story, as it was known to his community. It is also possible that the references to Jesus appearing in Galilee refer to Jesus' so-called 'second coming' (or *parousia*, as it is called in the New Testament).
2. The silence of the women is not necessarily permanent, but temporary.
3. There are several possible ways of explaining the fear of the women, which we will compare later on. Once again, the intelligent reader assumes that,

like their silence, the women's fear is temporary.
4. Mark's Gospel was the first to be written and does not need to conform to the pattern of later Gospels. In adding appearances in Galilee, Matthew (who seems to have used Mark as one of his major sources) may have been correcting Mark, just as he does when he adds the Sermon on the Mount (Matthew 5 to 7).
5. Mark may have had good reason for ending his Gospel so abruptly. What better way is there for a storyteller to draw the audience or the reader into the drama? Mark may be asking us to complete the Gospel with our own stories. There is no unbreakable rule that says that stories have to have nice, neat endings.

From this discussion, it is probable that our best option is to take Mark 16, verse 8 as it stands. We can be reasonably certain that it is the real ending of Mark's Gospel. Can we make sense of these verses and this story as it now is? What might Mark be trying to say to his community by concluding in such a way and what does he have to say to us, as modern readers of the Gospel? If we can come up with a plausible explanation of what Mark is doing in chapter 16, verses 1 to 8, then we have probably come a good distance towards solving the problem.

I. The story of the empty tomb
   Mark 16, verses 1 to 7

As we have seen, the women arrive at the empty tomb in the early morning and discover the stone rolled away and the presence of a young man clothed in white, seated inside the tomb (verses 1 to 5). Until their arrival, everything in the story has made sense. We know the women have a further role to play in regard to Jesus' burial, because of their vigilance at chapter 15, verse 47. We know that they have taken over the role of apostles from the Twelve who have long since fled.

Mark does not allow us to assume that in chapter 16 they are merely playing the role of women who are traditionally associated with rites of burial and mourning. For Mark, their actions have more significance than that. The language of chapter 15, verse 41 sets everything they do within the context of Christian discipleship and ministry. Their action in coming to the tomb is an act of faithfulness and ministry. However, as they reach the tomb (verse 3), their question shows that they have no apprehension of what has taken place.[4]

Their alarm at the stone being rolled away and the presence of the young man in white is therefore entirely comprehensible. Like Joseph, the women are taking a risk by being associated with the burial of a condemned criminal — one moreover executed on a charge of sedition — and they come in the early morning precisely to avoid detection.

They do not expect to encounter anyone (hence their problem in verse 3) and they have no desire to do so, given the suspect nature of what they are doing. Unlike Peter, they are prepared to be associated with a condemned man, but they are not prepared to court unnecessary risks. In the first place, their response to the young man is the very human fear of being discovered in what they are about to do.

The young man's white clothing, however, indicates that they have encountered no ordinary mortal. Elsewhere in Mark's Gospel, white is a heavenly symbol, a sign of the invasion of this world by that of another (like the transfiguration, where Jesus' garments are transformed to a dazzling white: chapter 9, verse 3). The description of the young man informs us that what is happening at the tomb is something which is beyond human experience.

The women's alarm betrays also this awareness. They, too, realise that they are somehow in the presence of a numinous reality. This is the first mention of the women's fear in the story. As we will see, the young man's words of reassurance and his message, far from allaying their fears, only intensify them.

The young man's message consists of four commands: 'do not be alarmed' (verse 6a), 'see' (verse 6b), 'go' (verse 7) and 'tell' (verse 7). They are encouraged to *overcome their fear* and to act as witnesses to the resurrection. In order to do so, they are invited to *see* the empty tomb which is the sign that points to the reality of the resurrection.

The New Testament gives us essentially two signs that point to the resurrection: the empty tomb and the appearances of the risen One. Paul makes no mention of the tradition of the empty tomb and focuses only on the appearances, including himself among those who saw the risen Lord (1 Corinthians chapter 15, verses 3 to 8). The Gospels of Matthew, Luke and John include both traditions of the empty tomb and the appearances (Matthew 28, Luke 24, John 20 and 21). Mark, however, gives us only the story of the empty tomb.

Note that these signs are not proofs of the resurrection, nor are they meant to be. They are addressed to faith. Those who witness Jesus' resurrection and his empty tomb in the Gospels are disciples: Jesus makes no appearance to unbelievers. As far as Mark is concerned, the empty tomb and the young man's words are enough to convince believers that Jesus has risen from the dead.

There is a problem, however, in interpreting the young man's message. Does it refer to the appearance of Jesus to Peter and the others — a story which Mark has chosen not to tell? Many would argue that this is so. In verse 7, the young man says of Jesus that 'he is going ahead of you to Galilee'. As we saw earlier, this fits in with Jesus' words to the disciples on the Mount of Olives: '[A]fter I am raised up, I will go before you to Galilee.' Those who argue for a lost ending to Mark's Gospel see this as a powerful argument in their favour. If Jesus promises to appear immediately after his resurrection, and if this promise is repeated by the angel at the empty tomb, then Mark ought to tell the story of Jesus' appearance.

There is another possibility, however, which I have already mentioned briefly: Jesus and the young man are referring not to a resurrection appearance, but to Jesus' 'appearance' (*parousia*) at the End. In that case, the words 'he will go before you to Galilee' refers to the pilgrimage of the Christian community as it journeys towards the Promised Land and the final Advent of God.

Galilee in the Gospel of Mark is the place of Jesus' ministry, his healing, teaching and welcoming of sinners. According to Isaiah chapter 9, verses 1 and 2, it is also the place of the gathering of the Gentiles (cf. Matthew 4, verses 13 to 16). In the first century AD, Jews and Gentiles lived in Galilee. It is thus a powerful symbol of the gathering in of God's people who are both Jew and Gentile. Jesus is going ahead of his church. He leads them towards the final consummation of all things. They are called to follow Jesus: to live as he lived, to love and liberate human beings from the bondage that imprisons them (whether that be physical, political or spiritual), to identify with human misery and to proclaim the reign of God.

If verse 8 is meant to be the ending of Mark's Gospel, the role that is given to the three women disciples in this proclamation is thus a crucial one. They are Mark's witnesses to the resurrection, just as they are the witnesses to the crucifixion. They are the ones who have seen Jesus crucified and seen the signs of his resurrection in the empty tomb. Not only so; they are also entrusted with the task of proclaiming the message of the resurrection to the other disciples.

The language here is the language of mission and preaching (proclamation): they are to *go* and *tell*. They, not the Twelve, are entrusted with the apostolic mission of the gospel. They are the ones who are to preach the good news, because only they have remained faithful. They are the witnesses to the Easter events — Good Friday as well as Easter Sunday — and they proclaim the future return of Jesus.

II. Fear and flight
Mark 16, verse 8

We have seen that fear is a major feature of this short chapter of Mark's Gospel. The women arrive in the half-light of early morning out of fear of being caught associating with a condemned man and they are afraid when they find the stone rolled from the mouth of the empty tomb and the awesome presence of the young man in white. At the end of the scene, they are so overcome by fear that they run away — 'for terror and amazement had seized them' (verse 8) — and keep silent.

Their initial fear at the beginning of the scene is understandable, as is also their fear when they reach the tomb and find things very different from what they have expected. But what about their fear at the end? How are we to understand it? Why does Mark end his Gospel this way?

Broadly speaking, there are two possible explanations for the fear and silence of the women at the end of the Gospel. The first explanation is that the women's fear and silence is an act of cowardice and disobedience in view of the young man's explicit commands.[5] Of the four commands, they disobey the two most important ones: they *see*, but do not *overcome* their fear; they *go*, but do not *tell*. This means that they have failed as disciples. In spite of being given the leading role in the drama, they spoil it by their failure. They fail both the mission and the proclamation which the heavenly messenger has given them. Their fear and their silence is the very opposite of faith.

According to this view, the women disciples end up in the same place as the men disciples. Just as the men flee at Jesus' arrest, symbolised in the flight of the naked young man (chapter 14, verses 50 to 52), so the women flee at the sight of the empty tomb. The faith of the male disciples fails at the point of Jesus' passion and death, whereas the faith of the female disciples fails at the point of his resurrection. Although the women are more faithful than the men in remaining with Jesus throughout his passion, with the message of the resurrection their faith, too, collapses. Finally, all disciples — whether female or male — are included in the same failure, the same human weakness and inability to respond to the gospel.

Like the men, the women disciples stand for the human condition. Their response is that of all human beings before the grace and power of God. Only faith, as a miracle from God, can enable Christians to understand and act faithfully. The disciples, male and female, represent the tragic reality of human frailty: the weakness of the flesh that wins out, despite the willingness of the spirit (chapter 14, verse 38).

In some ways this is an attractive and plausible reading of Mark's story which endeavours to make sense of the ending of the Gospel in verse 8. The reader is challenged by the failure of male and female disciples to respond in an entirely different way. We are to become aware of our human fragility, whether we are women or men, and ask God to give us the miracle of faith beyond human capabilities. Faith is a divine gift which comes to us precisely when we need it — when our own power and our own abilities give out.

Nevertheless, there are also problems with this view. It means that the Gospel ends on a tragic and depressing note: with the failure of all Jesus' disciples. It is hard to reconcile this with Mark's announcement at the very beginning of the Gospel that the story is to be 'good news' (chapter 1, verse 1).

Also it does not explain why the women are afraid at chapter 16, verse 8. If they have remained with him all through his crucifixion and have even taken the risk of going to the tomb to anoint his body with spices, why should they suddenly become afraid? The other disciples, after all, are plainly afraid of the authorities; the women have not allowed such fears to overcome them. So why do they flee?

Mark 14 presents Peter and the others as full of illusions about themselves, which is why they fail (chapter 14, verses 29 to 31). The women show no such illusion. Mark's only description of them presents them in in the highest of terms: they have been faithful to Jesus in both discipleship and in ministry (chapter 15, verse 41).

Moreover, it is not true to say that all disciples ultimately fail in their discipleship in Mark's Gospel. All the way through the Gospel, Mark has presented the 'little ones' — the poor, disabled and outcast — who understand, where often the inner group of disciples have failed (e.g. the leper in chapter 2, verses 40 to 45; the Syro-Phoeenician woman in chapter 5, verses 25 to 34; blind Bartimaeus in chapter 10, verses 46 to 52; the poor widow in chapter 12, verses 41 to 44). Significantly, women are an important part of this group in Mark's Gospel. In the passion narrative, the best example of this kind of faithful and perceptive discipleship which contrasts with the other disciples is, as we have seen, that of the woman of the anointing (chapter 14, verses 3 to 9). It makes sense that the story of Jesus' passion, death and resurrection concludes with the faithfulness of other women.

There is, however, another explanation which in my view makes more sense of the narrative. The women's reaction to the young man's message and the empty tomb is here not so much failure as a natural human reaction. The women's fear is not directed at the religious or secular authorities, but is rather the 'terror of the holy'.[6] Perhaps we today would prefer to call it 'awe'. The women are afraid precisely *because* they believe. They are overwhelmed by the reality of the resurrection and the awesome power of God which it displays. They are overcome with fear because an unheard-of event has occurred which is outside human experience and beyond human understanding. At the empty tomb, they find themselves on holy ground and they are so overcome by its holiness and power that they are terrified and flee.

Likewise, their silence could be seen to arise from the same motivation. Mark and his readers know well that the silence of the women, like their fear, is finally overcome. They do speak, they do proclaim the message of the gospel — otherwise how could the message have spread? At this point, however, they cannot speak.

There is a word in English which expresses perfectly this deep religious emotion: 'ineffable'. The word means literally 'not-able-to-be-spoken-about'. All of us have had experience of something that is ineffable. We try to describe it, but it is somehow beyond words; we keep faltering in our speech. Falling in love can be like that; giving birth is another such experience. Sometimes terrifying experiences are like that too: so painful and traumatic that they are beyond words to describe.

This is the experience of the women at the tomb. They are so overcome by the unexpected and awesome sight of the empty tomb that they cannot speak. Words cannot describe the awesome power and love of God which reveals itself in the worst of human tragedy and despair: 'Just as nothing can exceed the unspeakable tragedy and darkness of the passion, as recorded by St Mark, so nothing. . . can exceed, in his view, the ineffable wonder and mystery of its parallel or counterpart, the resurrection. The one unique event is answered by the other.'[7]

There are a number of parallels in the Bible for this kind of reaction to God's self-revelation.[8] At the giving of the Law on Mount Sinai, for example, the people are so terrified by the awesome presence of God that they do not want to speak to God (Exodus

20, verses 18 and 19). When he descends from the mountain, Moses' face is shining so brightly that the people are afraid to talk with him and he has to veil his face (Exodus 34, verses 29 to 34). Paul speaks of the mystical experience of 'a person in Christ' (presumably himself) who 'was caught up into paradise and heard things that are not to be told, that no mortal is permitted to repeat' (2 Corinthains 12, verse 4). This, too, refers to an ineffable experience — one which cannot be named, which is beyond the power of words.

More importantly, the reaction of the women has at least one very important parallel in Mark's Gospel. At Mark 4, verses 35 to 41, after the calming of the storm, we discover that the disciples are overwhelmed with fear: 'And they were filled with great fear and they said to one another, "Who then is this that even the wind and the sea obey him?" After the frightening storm, they experience a very different kind of fear. The fear for their lives has gone, but now a new fear has replaced it: the fear that is the natural response of human beings confronted by the holy mystery of God. Although this fear does not make them literally speechless, they have no real words with which to describe — let alone understand — the enigma of who Jesus is.

This is exactly the situation of the women at the empty tomb, though at a heightened level. The women's initial fear is for their lives, endangered by the vindictiveness and hatred of Jesus' enemies. The encounter with the young man and the empty tomb replaces their original fear with another, very different kind of fear. When faced with the awesome power and mystery of the God who raised Jesus from the dead, they are struck dumb. For the time being, they can do nothing but run from an experience which is so awe-inspiring.

So can we assume from this that the women finally break the silence in order to tell the story of the empty tomb and proclaim Christ's resurrection? At one level, we can assume that they do tell — otherwise Mark himself would not know the story. On another level, the level of the story, Mark does not answer our question. The narrative does not tell us whether the women overcome their fear and silence, and thus obey the heavenly messenger, or whether they are finally disobedient. There is a distinct note of ambiguity here which Mark makes no effort whatsoever to resolve.

But perhaps he does so for a very good reason. Mark now hands the story over to us. It is our decision which way the story will go. Everything depends on our response to the death and resurrection of Jesus. Will we, despite sharing the awe-struck response of the women, move on to proclaim his death and resurrection with our hearts, our lips, our lives? Or will we find some excuse to remain silent and inactive? The Gospel ends with a choice which challenges us either to embrace the good news, however awesome, or to reject it and sink back into apathy and indifference.

As St Paul recognised — and in this respect his theology is close to that of Mark — to embrace the message means that my life becomes radically Christ-shaped, formed by the experience of dying and rising (see Romans 6, verses 1 to 11): 'That which is Christ-like within us shall be crucified. It shall suffer and be broken. And that which is Christ-like within us shall rise up. It shall love and create.'[9]

Conclusion

The story of the empty tomb in Mark 16, verses 1 to 8 points us to the revelation of God in the death and resurrection of Jesus. Although for Mark this is good news, it is not the warm, reassuring message we might have preferred from Mark. On the contrary, Mark's Gospel ends on a note of fear and awe. It is particularly difficult for us modern Western Christians to understand this because we have lost almost all sense of the holy mystery of God. Lightfoot comments (and he was writing in the 1950s): 'One of the most obvious and disturbing phenomena in the religious life of Christendom during the last seventy or eighty years has been the disappearance of the awe or dread or holy fear of God.'[10]

Through his narrative of the resurrection, Mark reminds us of the awesome nature of God's power and God's action in the world. We are challenged out of our religious complacency, our over-familiarity with God. Too often we regard Jesus as a friend who exists to provide all our needs. Our prayer is a series of requests for ourselves and our families and friends which a nice, tame, friendly God will (hopefully) supply. Mark shatters these notions. In the women we see discipleship at its best — faithful, loving, caring — yet even they can neither stand nor speak before the breathtaking power of God.

The empty tomb points us away from our cosy, home-made God to a sense of the holy dread of God. We confront in Mark 16 the otherness of a God whose love and life are ineffable. Before that holy mystery made known to us in the Easter events, there is very little else we can do but keep silence. Ultimately in that silence and in that holy fear we will find life and healing.

A second important aspect of the story of the empty tomb is to do with discipleship. The abrupt ending at verse 8 challenges us to respond as true disciples to the message of the gospel. If we have a genuine vision of God's glory, it leads to an authentic following of Jesus. As the Christian community, we are given the message of the resurrection and called to proclaim it in both word and action. For Mark the resurrection means that 'Jesus is viewed as alive within the community and as continuing the same activities among them as he exercised among the original disciples. . . He leads the community.'[11]

With this challenge to follow the risen Lord, Mark draws us into the current of his narrative. As Myers points out, Mark's Gospel in this respect is rather like Michael Ende's novel, *The Never-Ending Story*, where the boy Bastian is drawn into becoming one of the characters in the book he is reading.[12] We, too, are drawn miraculously into the current of Mark's story. We become characters in the drama as the story becomes also our story.

Mark's strange abrupt ending serves an important function for us: it shapes us as disciples. The storyteller concludes his story by turning to us with a challenge: Will we follow Jesus into Galilee to proclaim God's loving and life-giving kingdom? Will we proclaim the good news of our crucified and risen Saviour through our life together in the church? Will we open our hearts to God's reign, living a life of prayer and reflection, embracing the conversion which lies at the heart of the gospel? Will we face the reality of death and open ourselves to God's searching love and forgiveness?

These are the questions with which Mark leaves us: to abandon the story or begin it all over again in our lives. The real ending of Mark's story rests not only with the women of Mark's empty tomb story, but also — indeed more importantly — with us:[13]

> God of terror and joy,
> you arise to shake the earth.

Open our graves and give us back the past;
so that all that has been buried
may be freed and forgiven,
and our lives may return to you
through the risen Christ. Amen.[14]

Discussion questions

Talking it through

1 Assuming that verse 8 is meant to be the ending of the book, how do you explain the role of the women? Is it another example of everything being turned upside down? What does this reveal about the nature of the gospel?

2 There are strong evidences of the supernatural in this chapter — the resurrection itself and the young man in white (an angel). Do you feel the supernatural is justified here, even though we don't see it much in everyday life?

Do you react to it in a similar way to the women? How do you react? Why?

3 What device does Mark seem to use, at the end of this section (chapter 16, verse 8), to involve the reader? What questions does it force you to ask yourself?

192/The resurrection of Jesus

4 What picture of God emerges in these eight verses? How does this picture come through?

5 What change has a study of Mark 11 to 16 made to you and your attitudes?

Widening our horizons

1 How would you differentiate between the supernatural and the natural? How would you apply this distinction to the following 'happenings':
(a) a particularly significant dream that answers a nagging problem?
(b) an apparently spontaneous cure of a serious, protracted health complaint?
(c) a mediator's success in bringing to an end a dispute of long standing?
(d) an adult conversion to Christianity?
Can we talk about different levels of meaning?

2 Is fear a good thing? What is it like in each of the following cases:
(a) awe of God?
(b) fear of the unknown?
(c) fear of a particular person?
How can fear be dealt with constructively in each case? Which of the three types of fear is for you the most dominant? Why?

3 How do each of the following contain elements of hope for you and where does that hope lie:
(a) the way God's agenda seems to be so different from that of our society?
(b) the ongoing power of Jesus' death and resurrection?
(c) the continuing existence and expansion of the Christian church, despite such influences as persecution, secularism and unbelief?

If you had to crystallise your belief system into one sentence, how would you complete the following:

'I have hope for the future because. . .'

Endnotes

Introduction

1. Martin Kähler, *The So-Called Historical Jesus and the Historical Biblical Christ*, Fortress, 1964, p.80
2. See R.H. Lightfoot, *The Gospel Message of St Mark*, Clarendon, 1950, pp.11–12.
3. For a helpful summary of the history of Markan studies in the modern era, see Morna D. Hooker, *The Gospel According to St Mark*, A.C. Black, 1991, pp.8–15.
4. On this, see Adela Yarbro Collins, *Is Mark's Gospel a Life of Jesus?*, Marquette University, 1990, pp.37–66, and Eduard Schweizer, *The Good News According to Mark*, SPCK, 1970, pp.21–23.
5. C.F.D. Moule, *The Gospel According to Mark*, Cambridge University Press, 1965, p.2
6. On the setting and background of Mark's Gospel, see the summary in Frank J. Matera, *What Are They Saying About Mark?*, Paulist, 1987, pp.1–17.
7. For a discussion of Mark's main reasons for writing, see D.E. Nineham, *Saint Mark*, Penguin, 1963, pp.30–35.
8. See Nineham, *Saint Mark*, pp.24–26, 35–38, 50–52.
9. Hooker, *St Mark*, p.26
10. Vincent Taylor (*The Gospel According to St Mark*, Macmil-

lan, 1952, pp.78–79) outlines the different types of stories and sayings in Mark's Gospel which took shape in the period of oral tradition.
11. For a defence of this view, see Martin Hengel, *Studies in the Gospel of Mark*, SCM, 1985, pp.50–53.
12. See John R. Donahue, 'From Passion Traditions to Passion Narrative' in *The Passion in Mark: Studies on Mark 14–16*, Werner H. Kelber (ed.), Fortress, 1976, pp.1–20.
13. For a brief summary of Mark's theological perspective, see Hooker, *St Mark*, pp. 19–26, and Schweizer, *Mark*, pp.380–386. See also Donald Senior, *The Passion of Jesus in the Gospel of Mark*, Michael Glazier, 1984, pp.139–158, for an outline of Mark's theology in the passion narrative.
14. On this theme, see Dietrich Bonhoeffer, *The Cost of Discipleship*, SCM, 1959, especially pp.76–83.
15. *Sing Alleluia*, Collins, 1987, No. 15

Chapter 1

1. Jack Dean Kingsbury, *Conflict in Mark: Jesus, Authorities, Disciples*, Fortress, 1989, pp.76–77
2. Schweizer, *Mark*, p.229
3. The donkey does not necessarily mean that Jesus is being humble. On the contrary, everywhere else in the Gospel he goes about on foot. Rather, the donkey is a symbol of peace as against war. See Hooker, *St Mark*, p.257.
4. Alexander the Great also rode into Jerusalem in 332 BC in triumph of a very different kind. Perhaps Mark is aware of this story and making a parody of it here.
5. Christopher Hope, 'Jerusalem: the Final Decision (Mark 11: 1 to 13: 37)' in *The Year of Mark*, H. McGinlay (ed.), Desbooks & JBCE, 1984, p.69
6. The word 'hosanna' is addressed to God and is literally

a cry for help: 'save now!' For Mark, however, it becomes a shout of praise. See Schweizer, *Mark*, pp.228–229.
7. What Jesus does is to enter the outer court of the Temple — the court of the Gentiles — and disrupt those who are trading in animals for sacrifice. He also disrupts those changing money from one currency to another, to enable pious Jews to pay the required Temple tax. For more on this, see Kingsbury, *Conflict in Mark*, pp.77–78.
8. Hooker, *St Mark*, p.262
9. On this, see Hooker, *St Mark*, pp.263–266.
10. See Kingsbury, *Conflict in Mark*, p.67.
11. Australian Hymn Book, Collins, 1977, No. 264

Chapter 2
1. Not burying someone was a terrible crime in the ancient world. The spirit of the dead person could not find rest until the proper burial rites had been completed.
2. 'The Gospel of Thomas' 65, in *The Other Gospels. Non-Canonical Gospel Texts*, R. Cameron (ed.), Westminster, 1982, p.33
3. On this see Nineham, *Saint Mark*, pp.310–311.
4. See Joachim Jeremias, *The Parables of Jesus*, SCM, 1972, pp.70–77. For a different view see Hooker, *St Mark*, pp.273–274.
5. The cornerstone may refer either to the foundation stone of a building or possibly the key stone of an arch. See Hooker, *St Mark*, p.277.
6. Bas van Iersel, *Reading Mark*, Liturgical Press, 1988, p.151
7. Schweizer, *Mark*, p.244
8. On this, see Ched Myers, *Binding the Strong Man: A Political Reading of Mark's Story of Jesus*, Orbis, 1990, pp.310–312.

9. Schweizer, *Mark*, pp.244–245
10. The story of the Book of Ruth centres around the practice of levirate marriage in the relationship between Ruth and Boaz.
11. In Matthew's interpretation of the story, it represents the third attempt to entrap Jesus: see Matthew 22, verse 34.
12. See Schweizer, *Mark*, pp.250–253.
13. Some theologians have argued that this is particularly (though not exclusively) the problem of women who suffer from low self-esteem more than from pride or selfishness. See the famous article by Valerie Saiving, 'The Human Situation: A Feminist View', in *Woman-Spirit Rising: A Feminist Reader in Religion*, Carol P. Christ and Judith Plaskow (eds), xxx, 1979, pp.25–42.
14. Herman C. Waetjen, *A Reordering of Power. A Socio-Political Reading of Mark's Gospel*, Fortress, 1989, p.193
15. See, for example, Acts 2, verses 34–35; 1 Corinthians 15, verse 25; and Hebrews 5, verse 60.
16. See, for example, Amos 2, verses 6 to 7; Amos 5, verses 11–12; Micah 2, verses 1–2, 8–9; and Micah 3, verses 1–3.
17. See Myers, *Binding the Strong Man*, pp.320–323, especially p.322.

Chapter 3

1. Kingsbury, *Conflict in Mark*, p.48
2. Nineham, *Saint Mark*, pp.339–343, and Augustine Stock, *Call to Discipleship: A Literary Study of Mark's Gospel*, Michael Glazier, 1982, pp.171–173
3. Hope, 'Jerusalem', pp.75–76
4. Archaeologists have recently discovered some of these stones in Jerusalem and they are indeed vast in size. See James H. Charlesworth, *Jesus within Judaism, New Light*

> from *Exciting Archaeological Discoveries*, SPCK, 1988, pp. 118–119.

5. In AD 40, the Roman Emperor Caligula tried to set up a statue of himself in the Temple in Jerusalem. The attempt failed because Caligula was assassinated.
6. Myers, *Binding the Strong Man*, pp.335–336
7. The early church historian Eusebius tells us that the Christians fled from Jerusalem in AD 66, just before the outbreak of the Jewish War. Mark possibly has this event in mind.
8. On Mark's use of this title for Jesus, see Hooker, *St Mark*, pp.88–93.
9. In the Old Testament, the title 'Son of God' refers simply to the king (see, for example, Psalm 2, verse 7), though clearly it takes on a deeper meaning in parts of the New Testament.
10. 'Parousia' actually means 'presence' or 'appearing'. The New Testament uses it as the technical term for what we sometimes call the 'second coming' of Jesus. The term is used by Paul and Matthew in particular, but the same concept is present in other parts of the New Testament, including Mark's Gospel. See Schweizer, *Mark*, pp.261–262, and H.K. McArthur, 'Parousia' in *The Interpreter's Dictionary of the Bible*, Vol. 3, pp.658–661. The term 'second coming' is not used in the New Testament.
11. For this view, see Lightfoot, *St Mark*, pp.48–49. See also Stock, *Call to Discipleship*, pp. 175–179
12. Senior, *Passion of Jesus*, pp.37–39, describes Mark 13 as the 'passion of the community' which corresponds to Jesus' own passion in the following chapters.
13. Schweizer, *Mark*, p.277

Chapter 4

1. This seems to consist only of the Twelve (verse 17), but there are other indications of a wider group, including the young disciple mentioned at Mark 14, verse 51. It suggests the probability that there were more disciples than just the Twelve present at the Last Supper. If so, certainly the women who followed Jesus from Galilee would have been included among them (Mark 15, verses 40 to 41). See Dorothy A. Lee, 'Presence or Absence? The Question of Women Disciples at the Last Supper', *Pacifica* 6 (1, 1993), pp.1–20.
2. Francis J. Moloney, *A Body Broken for a Broken People: Eucharist in the New Testament*, Collins Dove, 1990, p.31
3. See, for example, Elisabeth Schüssler Fiorenza, *In Memory of Her: A Feminist Theological Reconstruction of Christian Origins*, SCM, 1983, pp. xii-xiv.
4. This may be a continuation of Mark's theme of Jesus eating with 'tax collectors and sinners' and consorting with the sick and unclean (Mark 2, verses 15 to 17).
5. As Senior points out in *Passion of Jesus* p.45, almsgiving — that is, the giving of charity — was considered a sacred duty for Jewish people, particularly during Passover. See also Hooker, *St Mark*, p.329: 'The woman's service to Jesus is as much a "good work" as the almsgiving her critics advocate.'
6. See Mary Ann Tolbert, 'Mark' in *The Women's Bible Commentary*, Carol A. Newsom and Sharon H. Ringe (eds), SPCK, 1992, pp.270–271
7. Ralph P. Martin, *Mark: Evangelist and Theologian*, Paternoster, 1972, pp.202, 212
8. Senior, *Passion of Jesus*, p.48
9. Hooker, *St Mark*, p.330
10. Further on this, see Schüssler Fiorenza, *In Memory of Her*,

and Senior, *Passion of Jesus*, p.47
11. On the problem of the Last Supper as a Passover meal and the difficulties of reconciling this with John's dating, see Schweizer, *Mark*, pp.294–297, and Hooker, *St Mark*, pp.332–334.
12. The word 'eucharist' to describe the Lord's Supper comes from the Greek verb 'to give thanks'. The verb is found in this passage in verse 23: 'Then he took the cup and after *giving thanks* he gave it to them. . .' It parallels the *blessing* of the loaf of bread in verse 22.
13. For more information on this aspect of Jesus' ministry, see Joachim Jeremias, *New Testament Theology*, SCM, 1971, pp.114–121.
14. See Schweizer, *Mark*, pp.304 and 305.
15. On this theme, see Moloney, *A Body Broken*, especially pp.19–35 and 121–137.

Chapter 5

1. See Senior, *Passion of Jesus*, p.15.
2. Dennis M. Sweetland, *Our Journey with Jesus*, Michael Glazier, 1987, pp.77–78
3. Ralph P. Martin, *Mark: Evangelist and Theologian*, Paternoster, 1972, p.119
4. Moule, *Mark*, p.117. See also Schweizer, *Mark*, p.315.
5. See Hooker, *St Mark*, pp.346–347.
6. Senior, *Passion of Jesus*, pp.77–80
7. See above, chapter 3, pp.42, 56–58.
8. See Mary Ann Tolbert, *Sowing the Gospel: Mark's World in Literary-Historical Perspective*, Fortress, 1989, pp.216–217.
9. On this theme, see D.A. Lee-Pollard, 'Powerlessness as Power: A Key Emphasis in the Gospel of Mark', in *Scottish Journal of Theology*, 40 (2, 1987), pp.173–188.

10. For a helpful introduction to this scene, see Nineham, *Saint Mark*, pp.393–395.
11. On the role of Judas Iscariot in Mark's passion story, see Stock, *Call to Discipleship*, pp.194–196.
12. See H. Fleddermann, 'The Flight of a Naked Young Man (Mark 14: 51–52)', in *Catholic Biblical Quarterly* (3, 1979), pp.412–418. See also Myers, *Binding the Strong Man*, pp.368–369.
13. Leonard Cohen, *Book of Mercy*, Jonathan Cape, 1984, No.48

Chapter 6

1. See Hooker, *St Mark*, p.362 and Senior, *Passion of Jesus*, pp.100–101.
2. E. Schweizer, *The Good News According to Mark*, SPCK, 1970, p.330
3. See above, chapter 3, pp.52–55
4. D. Senior, *The Passion of Jesus in the Gospel of Mark*, Michael Glazier, 1987, p.142
5. M.A. Tolbert, *Sowing the Gospel: Mark's World in Literary-Historical Perspective* Fortress, 1989, p.278
6. On this point and on the more general issue of what actually happened at Jesus' trial, see Schweizer, *Mark*, pp.321–328.
7. D.E. Nineham, *Saint Mark*, Penguin, 1963, pp.399–400
8. On this theme, see Frank J. Matera, *Passion Narratives and Gospel Theologies. Interpreting the Synoptics through their Passion Stones*, Paulist, 1986, pp.38–39, 43–44, 51–59.
9. C. Myers, *Binding the Strong Man: A Political Reading of Mark's Story of Jesus*, Orbis, 1990, p.373
10. Flogging was carried out with a leather whip that had pieces of metal attached to it; it tore the skin to the bone. See Schweizer, *Mark*, p.338

Chapter 7

1. Senior, *Passion of Jesus*, 116, thinks that verse 21 ('to carry his cross') suggests to the alert reader that Simon is acting as a true disciple in carrying his cross. Of course, it is Jesus' cross he carries and not his own, but they are not entirely separate.
2. For more information on crucifixion, see Martin Hengel, *Crucifixion in the Ancient World and the Folly of the Message of the Cross*, SCM, 1977, especially pp.22–32.
3. At Matthew 24, verse 34, the wine is mixed with 'gall' (vinegar) which Matthew sees as part of the mocking of Jesus, in line with Psalm 26, verse 21. See Senior, *Passion of Jesus*, p.117.
4. Compare Luke's rather different picture of the response of the two bandits (Luke 23, verses 39 to 43): while one of them mocks Jesus, the other turns to him in repentance. Luke presents Jesus still saving people and welcoming them into the kingdom even as he dies.
5. Ralph P. Martin, *Mark: Evangelist and Theologian*, Paternoster, 1972, p.120
6. See R.H. Lightfoot, *The Gospel Message of St. Mark*, p.55
7. As Senior argues (*Passion*, pp.126–129)
8. See Lightfoot, *St Mark*, pp.55–56.
9. See Nineham, *Saint Mark*, p.430 and Schweizer, *Mark*, p.355.
10. Although the Greek could be translated, 'Truly this man was *a* son of God', it is unlikely that this is the meaning intended by Mark.
11. The account in Matthew 27, verse 54 indicates that, when the centurion and others 'saw the earthquake and what took place', they called Jesus God's Son. No attempt will be made here to explain the differing accounts in Mark and Matthew. Mark's account must, I feel, be allowed

not only to stand, but to be given the full significance he appears to have intended it to have.
12. J. Moltmann, *The Crucified God*, SCM, 1974, p.51
13. Hans-Ruedi Weber, *The Cross: Tradition and Interpretation*, Eerdmans, 1978, p.109, sees the centurion's recognition as a miracle, indeed *the* miracle of the crucifixion: 'When the story of Jesus appears to have reached its ignominious end, the miracle happens: an outsider, a pagan, sees what has really occurred.'
14. Senior, *Passion*, 135
15. Quoted from Dietrich Bonhoeffer in Hans-Ruedi Weber, *On a Friday Noon: Meditations under the Cross*, World Council of Churches, 1979, p.30.
16. Bruce Dawe, 'And a Good Friday Was Had by All', in *Sometimes Gladness, Collected Poems, 1954–1987*, Longman Cheshire, 1988, p.38
17. Gerald O'Collins, *The Calvary Christ*, SCM, 1977, p.115

Chapter 8

1. See Nineham, *Saint Mark*, p.440.
2. For a list of the problems, see Lightfoot, *St Mark*, p.85.
3. Schweizer is an example of a commentator who takes the view that the ending of Mark's Gospel was accidentally lost (*Mark*, pp.365–367).
4. Schweizer, *Mark*, p.371, sees the picture of a huge stone sealing the tomb as a symbol of human mortality. For human beings 'the large stone closes the tomb now and forever, and this makes the miraculous intervention of God which has already occurred [in verse 4] so much more impressive.'
5. For this view of the women's response in verse 8, see for example John D. Crossan, 'Empty Tomb and Absent Lord

(Mark 16: 1–8)' in *The Passion in Mark: Studies on Mark 14–16*, W.H. Kelber (ed.), Fortress, 1976, p.149. There are also two articles that discuss the question in detail, giving the same view that the women's response puts them on the same level of failure and disobedience as the men. See T.E. Boomershine, 'Mark 16: 8 and the Apostolic Commission', *Journal for Biblical Literature*, 100 (2, 1981) pp.225–239 and T.E. Boomershine and G.L. Bartholomew, 'The Narrative Technique of Mark 16: 8' in the same issue of the same journal, pp.213–223.

6. For this explanation, see especially the very fine essay of Lightfoot, 'St Mark's Gospel: Complete or Incomplete?' in *St Mark*, pp.80–97. See also Senior, *Passion of Jesus*, p.137.
7. Lightfoot, *St Mark*, p.89
8. See Nigel Watson, 'The Story of the Resurrection in Mark' in *The Year of Mark*, Hugh McGinlay (ed.), p.17.
9. Leunig, *A Common Prayer*, Collins Dove, 1990
10. Lightfoot, *St Mark*, p.97
11. Ernest Best, *Mark: The Gospel as Story*, T.&T. Clark, 1983, p.76
12. Myers, *Binding the Strong Man*, p.449; see pp.448–450
13. On this view of Mark's ending see Myers, *Binding the Strong Man*, pp.400–401.
14. Janet Morley, *All Desires Known*, Movement for the Ordination of Women, 1988, p.16

Bibliography

Useful commentaries on Mark

C.E.B. Cranfield, *The Gospel According to Saint Mark*, Cambridge University, 1959
A solid, conservative commentary on Mark's Gospel, based on the Greek text.

Robert A. Guelich, *Mark* (2 volumes), Word, 1989
This commentary is written from a critical, evangelical perspective and gives a scholarly reading of Mark's Gospel. The second volume is not yet published. It is based on the Greek text, but with English translation.

Morna D. Hooker, *The Gospel According to St Mark*, A.& C. Black, 1991
A scholarly commentary on Mark's Gospel by an experienced English scholar, based on the author's own translation. It is one of the best recent commentaries on Mark.

C.F.D. Moule, *The Gospel According to Mark*, Cambridge University, 1965
A short, readable commentary on Mark, based on the New English Bible.

Ched Myers, *Binding the Strong Man: A Political Reading of Mark's Story*, Orbis, 1990
A political reading of Mark's Gospel which challenges more

traditional readings and for that reason is worth reading. It tends, however, to impose its own ideology onto Mark's Gospel in a way which is not always convincing.

D.E. Nineham, *Saint Mark*, Penguin, 1963
Generally regarded as the standard commentary on Mark's Gospel. It is scholarly and informative, dealing with a number of important critical issues.

Eduard Schweizer, *The Good News According to Mark*, SPCK, 1970
This fine commentary has already become a 'classic' in studies on Mark. The translation is based on the TEV (Good News for Modern Man).

Vincent Taylor, *The Gospel According to St Mark*, Macmillan, 1952
Although ageing, this still remains an excellent commentary on Mark, particularly for background questions on the Gospel's form and formation.

Useful investigations of key ideas in Mark

Paul J. Achtemeier, *Mark*, Fortress, 1975
A short but well-written overview of Mark's Gospel, with a focus on preaching from the Gospel.

Ernest Best, *Mark: The Gospel as Story*, T.&T. Clark, 1983
A good introduction to many of the critical and theological issues of Mark's Gospel.

James H. Charlesworth, *Jesus within Judaism: New Light from Exciting Archaeological Discoveries*, SPCK, 1988
A very readable book, which explains recent research into the life and environment of Jesus, based on the findings of archaeology.

Adela Yarbro Collins, *Is Mark's Gospel a Life of Jesus?* Marquette University, 1990
This scholarly lecture discusses the genre of Mark's Gospel and considers the question of its relationship to history. The author stresses Mark's apocalyptic character.

Elisabeth Schüssler Fiorenza, *In Memory of Her: A Feminist Theological Reconstruction of Christian Origins*, SCM, 1983
A ground-breaking examination of the role of women in the New Testament and in the early church. Parts II and III give a particularly helpful overview of the New Testament in relation to women.

Sean Freyne, *Galilee, Jesus and the Gospels*, Fortress, 1988
This book focuses on the role of Galilee in the Gospels, examining the socio-political situation and background of Galilee. There is a helpful chapter on Galilee in Mark's Gospel.

Daniel J. Harrington, *Interpreting the New Testament: A Practical Guide*, Michael Glazier, 1979
An introduction to the critical tools used by scholars in reading the Gospels. It is readable and, while dealing with technical concepts, uses non-technical language to explain them.

Martin Hengel, *Studies in the Gospel of Mark*, SCM, 1985
Written by a well-known German scholar, this book argues for the more traditional view of Mark as written in Rome under the influence of Peter.

Howard Clark Kee, *Community of the New Age: Studies in Mark's Gospel*, SCM, 1977
A scholarly study of Mark which stresses the importance of apocalyptic and community in understanding the background to the Gospel and its theology.

Jack Dean Kingsbury, *Conflict in Mark: Jesus, Authorities, Disciples*, Fortress, 1989
A short, readable study of the theme of conflict in Mark's Gospel.

The Passion in Mark. Studies on Mark 14–16, Werner H. Kelber (ed.), Fortress, 1976
A collection of articles on Mark's passion narrative by a number of American scholars. The focus of the articles is on Mark's theological perspective which emerges throughout the narrative.

Lee, Dorothy A., 'Presence or Absence? The Question of Women Disciples at the Last Supper', *Pacifica* 6 (1993), pp.1–20.
A study of the Last Supper in the four Gospels and Paul, arguing that it is probable that women disciples were present, along with the Twelve and others, at the Last Supper.

D.A. Lee-Pollard, 'Powerless as Power: A Key Emphasis in the Gospel of Mark', *Scottish Journal of Theology* 40 (2, 1987), pp.173–188
A study of Mark's understanding of power and its radical meaning in relation to the cross and Jesus' call to powerlessness.

R.H. Lightfoot, *The Gospel Message of St Mark*, Clarendon, 1950
Contains eight essays on Mark's Gospel, including a study of the ending of the Gospel. Though written in 1950, this beautiful book is well ahead of its time.

Elizabeth Struthers Malbon, *Narrative Space and Mythic Meaning in Mark*, JSOT Press, 1991
A structural reading of Mark's narrative, focussing on Mark's use of geography. In particular, the book studies the way in which Mark understands categories of space.

Ralph P. Martin, *Mark: Evangelist and Theologian*, Paternoster, 1972
A good and scholarly study of Mark's theology and the context out of which it comes, written from an evangelical perspective.

Frank J. Matera, *Passion Narratives and Gospel Theologies: Interpreting the Synoptics through Their Passion Stories*, Paulist, 1986
As the title suggests, a comparative study of the passion narratives in each of the first three Gospels. In each section, the book gives an overview of a Gospel, followed by more detailed commentary and concluding with theological reflection.

Frank J. Matera, *What Are They Saying about Mark?*, Paulist, 1987

A helpful overview of current scholarly views of Mark's Gospel on a number of critical, theological and literary issues. Short and easy to read.

J. Moltmann, *The Crucified God*, SCM, 1974
Written by a leading German systematic theologian, this is a powerful theological presentation of the theology of the cross.

Gerald O'Collins, *The Calvary Christ*, SCM, 1977
A readable work on New Testament understandings of the cross, written by a systematic theologian.

David Rhoads and Donald Michie, *Mark as Story: An Introduction to the Narrative of a Gospel*, Fortress, 1982
A readable study of Mark's Gospel from a literary perspective. The book begins with a contemporary and fairly colloquial translation of the Gospel without verse or chapter divisions.

Donald Senior, *The Passion of Jesus in the Gospel of Mark*, Michael Glazier, 1987
An excellent and readable study of Mark's passion narrative (chapters 14 to 15), setting it within the wider framework of Mark's narrative and theology.

Augustine Stock, *Call to Discipleship: A Literary Study of Mark's Gospel*, Michael Glazier, 1987
A readable study of discipleship in Mark's Gospel and how it relates to other Markan themes.

Denis M. Sweetland, *Our Journey with Jesus: Discipleship According to Mark*, Michael Glazier, 1987
A readable study of discipleship in Mark's Gospel and how it relates to other Markan themes.

Gerd Theissen, *The Shadow of the Galilean*, SCM, 1987
An unusual study of the historical Jesus, which uses a first-person narrative form and sets the whole in the context of an imaginary character. Absorbing reading, based on good scholarship.

Mary Ann Tolbert, 'Mark', *The Womens's Bible Commentary*, Carol A. Newsome and Sharon H. Ringe (eds.), SPCK, 1992, pp.263–274
This study of Mark focuses on the role played by women in the Gospel, dealing with each example in turn. It concludes with a discussion of women disciples in the passion narrative.

Mary Ann Tolbert, *Sowing the Gospel: Mark's World in Literary-Historical Perspective*, Fortress, 1989
An important scholarly examination of Mark's literary character, which focuses on the parable of the sower.

The Year of Mark, Hugh McGinlay (ed.), Desbooks & JBCE, 1984
A collection of articles on Mark's Gospel, written in a very readable style by a number of Australian scholars.

Useful treatments of present-day faith and life issues raised in Mark

Boff, Leonardo, *Jesus Christ Liberator*, SPCK, 1990
An examination in some depth of the need for liberation from the sins of modern society

Bonhoeffer, Dietrich, *The Cost of Discipleship*, SCM, 1959
Bonhoeffer's most famous book which arose out of his opposition to Nazism in the 1930s and his perception that the church as a whole was offering 'cheap grace'. The centrepiece of the book is a study of the Sermon on the Mount.

Gill, Athol, *Life on the Road*, Herald Press, 1989
Examines discipleship as revealed in the Gospels: the call, the cost, the place of possessions, the nature of community and mission, the role of prayer and grace.

Kavanagh, John, *Following Christ in a Consumer Society*, Orbis, 1991
Contrasts the lifestyle advocated in the Gospels and that of modern Western society.

Francis J. Moloney, *A Body Broken for a Broken People: Eucharist in the New Testament*, Collins Dove, 1990
Written by an Australian New Testament scholar, the book argues that the Lord's Supper in the New Testament is offered not for the righteous, but for those whose lives are broken and fragmented.

Henri Nouwen, *Reaching Out: The Three Movements of the Spiritual Life*, Doubleday, 1975
A book on spirituality which focuses on the movement from loneliness to solitude, from hostility to hospitality, and from illusion to prayer. These movements exemplify, in a spiritual context, Mark's understanding of losing one's life in order to find it.

Charles Ringma, *Seize the Day with Dietrich Bonhoeffer*, Albatross, 1991
365 reflections in the form of 'conversations' between the author and Bonhoeffer that brings out key themes in Mark's Gospel.

Paul Tournier, *The Strong and the Weak*, SCM, 1963
The author argues against classifying people into strong and weak. Rather, he sees God taking us as we are and working with us.

Jon Sobrino, *Christology at the Crossroads*, SCM, 1978
A theological study of the theology of the cross from the perspective of a liberation theologian.

Hans-Ruedi Weber, *On a Friday Noon: Meditations under the Cross*, World Council of Churches, 1979
This is a book designed for Lenten meditations on the cross. It consists of paintings and texts from various sources.

Yoder, John Howard, *The Politics of Jesus*, Eerdmans, 1972
The author shows how the teaching and ministry of Jesus represents a coherent and relevant approach to Christian behaviour today.

Wallis, Jim, *The Call to Conversion*, Lion, 1981
The author interprets the Christian conversion experience as applying to all of life.

Notes

Notes

Notes

Notes

Notes

Notes

Notes